Flying with Eagles

By

John Haynes

ENJOY THE BOOK PAM,
"SUCCESS BREEDS SUCCESS"
YOUR A SPECIAL PERSON

John
x

"Part inspiration and part learning from his, and other peoples, mistakes and successes. This book can become your roadmap for improvement."

"A remarkably visionary writer, John has written this book which identifies many specific actions you should take for your business and your personal life."

Buy the book, read it, then get busy!

CONTENTS

FOREWORD

All the business success in the universe isn't worth leaving your family for every morning if it doesn't produce financial results for the people you love. And that's what John Haynes does; he develops people to be excellent in their business and private lives.

John has worked in the self-development area for more than fifty years. He has learnt, grown, made big mistakes and gone through 'the dark night of the soul' to get where he is today. With his desire for personal development after leaving school at 14½, he is now the Managing Director of The International Coaching Academy, and was, previously the Regional Director of a large company in control of 1500 people.

He has travelled to many countries sharing his knowledge and skills, including India, the USA, Australia, Africa, The Emirates, Europe and South Africa.

He has helped hundreds of thousands of people worldwide to achieve their goals dreams and financial security.

John now is assisting businesses, universities and individuals who have no self-confidence to reach new levels of success, and live up to their full potential.

Now companies in all industries can get on the Master's Programme to help them become more focused, have better strategies, better planning, more powerful marketing and sales approaches, and higher profits. Readers will discover the practical techniques that the most successful businesses use to thrive, even in the toughest markets.

They'll also learn how to achieve their business's vision, values, mission, purpose, and goals—both short and long-term.

Remember, it's not where you are coming from that matters; it is where you are going.

Hire the best people --and motivate them to excellence.

John Haynes will show how any company and any person, can create a strategy that gets its business reaching its full potential.

1. LIFE ONLY GETS BETTER WHEN YOU GET BETTER

'Work is an extension of personality. It is achievement. It is one of the ways in which a person defines himself, measures his worth and his humanity.' Peter Drucker.

We all have brilliant memories, but we are never taught how to use them properly. Your subconscious mind is like a huge memory bank. Its capacity is virtually unlimited. It permanently stores everything that happens to you. By the age of 21 we have already permanently stored one hundred times the contents of the entire Encyclopaedia Britannica. Your unconscious memory is virtually perfect.

You can remember things in detail if the memory has a strong emotional presence. You surely remember your first kiss, your first job and car, the saddest time in your life, perhaps even a boss from hell? If a memory is filled with strong emotion, your brain will remember it.

Perhaps my most memorable moment came the day after I left school when my mother excitedly told me that she had gotten me a job at the Hygena factory where she worked as a pastry cook. I'm guessing that when she asked the bosses whether there was a place for me, it was something of a no brainer seeing how they were obviously keen to keep on my mother's good side – they loved her pies and scones that much. I was to take up a position as an apprentice cabinet maker.

So, there I was at the tender age of 14½ working in a factory. Was this the job I had dreamed of? In hindsight, had I even had a dream job in mind? I'm quite sure that if I had, it wasn't a cabinet maker. It certainly wasn't a role that was suited to my skills and abilities. As Abraham Maslow explained, our main function in life is to self-actualise – to find a career that makes our inner music play. This work should be suited to your own unique abilities. A cabinet maker? Me? Never. I was the sort of kid who couldn't put a lightbulb in without darkening the whole street. It is said that when you find a job you love; you will never work another day in your life. It is also said that an investment in yourself is the greatest investment of all. Most people, like me at the time, never invest in themselves; i.e. education and skills, after I was asked to leave school when I was 14½ and because I wasn't interested in investing in me.

The More You Learn, the More You Earn

If only I had known this valuable knowledge then. Just one year of additional education could add £200,000 to your income. It's also thought that by studying the right subjects, you can increase your earnings potential by between ten and 20 per cent each year. Of course, I had barely invested five minutes in my education, a fact that reminds me of an analogy a good friend told me about. He said that you could tell how high a building will become by looking at the depth of its foundations. Once a building is complete, the builders cannot go back and decide to add an extra five or ten floors to the structure by digging deeper foundations. It is not physically possible. A similar principle applies to humans but with one brilliant exception. You can tell how high a person will rise in life by how deeply they dig their foundations of practical skills and knowledge, but unlike a building, a person can continually deepen their foundations – the extent of their knowledge – by simply learning more. There are no limits.

Those few words gave me so much encouragement and still continue to do so, but I was yet to benefit from my friend's wisdom when I was starting out at the factory. Even if I had, I wonder if I would have fully understood their significance. As

I started my new job, I remember the foreman, the formidable Old Ernie, telling me I was the 'Can Lad'. I was to clock on at 8 am as the hooter sounded each morning and work overtime until 7 pm every night except Fridays. On Saturdays, I was to work between 8 am and 1 pm, and he would let me know if I was needed on Sundays. And that was that. I was serving an apprenticeship in something I wasn't really interested in and putting in extraordinarily long hours as I did. That habit of hard labour has never left me and has instead given me a sense of discipline that so many folks lack. Putting a lad of 14½ to work such long days would never be tolerated in modern society but, for me, it forged a habit of going the extra mile, and putting more in without getting much out.

Factory Life

I quickly learned the rules of factory life, recognising that the most important of all was never to cross Old Ernie. Although I wasn't very good at my job and there was no way there was any music playing inside me, I found the comradeship at the factory endearing. I was part of a rough, but caring, family who looked after their own. The factory was cold and gloomy, but fun, mischief and mickey-taking were all appealing. The older fellas saw me as a son in a way and wasted no time in assigning me to look-out duties. My labour gang would regularly down tools for a quick game of cards and instructed me to give three quick taps of my hammer at the sight of Old Ernie. It was an easy job because I could often hear Ernie coming even before I could see him. He had a habit of humming as he strode the factory floor, a stern angry hum that could mean big trouble was just around the corner. The sound of my hammer banging three times in quick succession meant that a lot of that potential trouble was avoided. He was a good bloke, Old Ernie, firm but fair not hard and cold as his demeanour would suggest. He would often give me a nod that signified I could leave work at 6.45 pm instead of

7 pm. It was just 15 minutes; but felt like an age at the end of a long working day, and I was always grateful to him. I was learning the principles of hard work alongside scouse humour and strong comradeship.

Today, I feel fortunate to have been surrounded by such honest, hardworking people in my youth.

Your Reference Group

I now know that it is imperative that we spend time around the right sort of people – people with good and honest intentions. We must avoid toxic people – those who complain, condemn and criticise all the time. These negative people depress you, affecting your mind and taking all the fun out of living. The people around you have an inordinate influence on your own personality, your opinions, your future and your goals. My reference group was Harry the Horse, Lenny the Animal, Slippery, Sad Jim, Slick Nick, Bob the Slob, Sly Eye, Johnny No Mates – and many others. Good or bad, these were the people I looked up to. The job was hard, and it made me feel tired for much of my time. My mum and dad spurred me on, my mum usually by sneaking me cakes and scones that were meant for the directors. She told me she was doing them a favour as her baking was causing them to put on weight. I started to pick up skills as a cabinet maker, but I knew it wasn't what I wanted from life.

However, I never became so good at the job that the feeling that an ambulance was needed on permanent standby should I do any permanent damage to myself ever left me. I rarely felt happy on the inside. Working with my hands didn't come naturally to me, and I still remember Little Sam taking a quick sip from his flask every time I picked up a saw.

Self-Actualise

It was Abraham Maslow, the transpersonal psychologist, who wrote that the goal of human life is to become everything you can be, going on to say that a human's purpose should be to fulfil their potential and to accomplish something wonderful in their life.

Your aim should be to get the best from yourself in every area of your life. It is said that the people who self-actualise and find their music inside go on to accomplish an extraordinary amount – as opposed to the great majority who accomplish very little. It became my opinion years later that these peak performers or self-actualisers earn more money, have better relationships, are happier, enjoy greater successes and live a longer life. So say the many surveys, and experts around the world.

Thus, finding a job that you love must surely be one of your important goals in life. Of course, I didn't understand all this at the time. All I understood was that I had to work extremely hard and try to cover up the many mistakes I made – otherwise I would run the risk of Old Ernie's hum becoming very stern indeed. I wonder now whether parents and the schools and universities do their best to help youngsters find their music inside or whether these kids are simply pushed into a career that is not necessarily the best for them. I struggle with the idea that there are so many people who are unhappy in their work and go home each night to moan and watch TV simply because they haven't been taught about the importance of self-actualisation.

The Beatles

My world of quiet desperation at the factory continued at the same pace as it always did, but a change was coming, and one that would not just affect me but would affect the entire city of Liverpool. Four young lads formed a band called the Silver Beatles, a name that was later shortened to simply; The Beatles. Their wild and loud music was unlike anything we had ever heard before, and the city came to light as a result of their uplifting tunes. I first saw them in a venue called the Cavern Club on Mathew Street, although my mate Kenny had taken me there in pursuit of the singer's pretty fans as opposed to the music.

The Beatles helped me and the lads from the factory shake off our dark days. The Beatles sang with passion and belief – they had truly found their music inside – and were sharing it with the city. As a result, the city came alive. The group became our heroes, our role models. If four scruffy lads from Liverpool could love life so much, then so could we. When the group had their first number one, Please Please Me, it was as if the city had won the world cup. We went mad with pride in the factory and couldn't wait for the bus journey home, after the pub, when both decks of the bus would be filled with the sound of the workers singing the latest songs. It became such a ritual that purchasing a return ticket and travelling back and forth, at night, for a while became the new norm. Even Old Ernie's hum took on a jollier note. The sense of energy was inspiring.

The Beatles helped me to eliminate my otherwise negative thoughts from my mind. I have since found that our ability to keep our minds on what we want and off what we don't want determines our levels of positivity, happiness and health. The more you talk about the people and situations that make you angry and upset, the angrier and more upset you become. Negative emotions depress your mind and body, robbing you of energy and lessening the strength of your immune system, making you more susceptible to illnesses of all kinds. Because I was always criticising myself for being in a job, I was rubbish at, feeling tired and discouraged was the way of life. My job was undermining my confidence and enthusiasm. I have since found out that one unrestrained outburst of anger can consume as much as three hours of regular work. I was letting Old Ernie and my workmates down.

The Law of Substitution

If only I had been educated enough back then. But it wasn't until years later when I spent time with a mentor that I discovered that the best way to avoid the temptation to complain and criticise was to use the Law of Substitution. It was drummed into me that your conscious mind can only hold one thought at a time. Thus, you can cancel out a negative thought by replacing it with a positive thought. You can literally neutralise the emotions of anger, fear and worry with a strong affirmation – I am responsible, I like myself, or I am the best, and many more. When you feel yourself getting angry and before giving yourself the chance to have regrets about what you are about to say later, repeat under your breath 'I am responsible, I am responsible, I am responsible'. You cannot accept responsibility for a situation and continue to be angry at the same time.

Blame triggered my own negative emotions. Anger and resentment almost always require you to blame others for something. I blamed the government, the directors of Hygena, the Union and my old mum for putting me in a job I was useless at. If it wasn't for the comradeship and friendship of my workers, I think I would have gone under at that early age. I later found that the instant that you are able to stop blaming others and start taking responsibility, you have a greater degree of control in your own life. You begin to think clearly and start to solve your problems in a civilised way. There's an old saying that tells us we are mentally healthy to the exact degree that we can freely forgive anyone who has hurt us. My mentor, years later, had me write out a list of all the people who had angered me in the past. I was able to cancel out any upsetting feelings about those people simply by saying 'I forgive you,' as I read through that list. You cannot forgive and continue to be upset. The Beatles' music helped us to use the Law of Substitution by helping us to tune out the negative thoughts in favour of the positive ones we gained from singing their songs. You can only have one thought at a time, and every time we sang in the factory or on the bus home, our only feelings were positive.

It wasn't long before a new role model was to come into my life – the famous football manager of Liverpool football club – Mr Bill Shankly.

I believe that the role models I had followed - Bill Shankly, Nelson Mandela and Mother Theresa - all had three primary virtues: prudence, justice and benevolence.

- Prudence means that you think honestly about what you say and do, how to deal with different types of people and how to conduct yourself in every situation.
- Justice means standing up for the people who you feel to be on the side of fair play and avoiding the urge to be influenced by power or money.
- Benevolence means to be at your happiest when making a positive difference in the lives of other people.

Mandela, Shankly and Mother Theresa along with the Beatles, had given me hope in my heart, to the extent that my dark days were becoming lighter. Shankly and The Beatles were, for me, a life changer.

Bill Shankly

Bill Shankly, an idol of mine, took Liverpool from the abyss of the old second division to their first-ever FA Cup in 1965. Until then, I had been a staunch Everton blue but Shankly, with his motivational words, seemed to inspire not only me but the whole city. So, there I was, an Evertonian in the Kop, singing along to the Beatles with my former sporting enemies - We all loved to sing, 'She Loves You Yeah, Yeah, Yeah'.

At the end of the game, Shankly walked out onto the pitch with his clenched fist making the supporters feel like we were a true part of the team. His philosophy reached into the souls of every one of us, raising our hopes that were about to embark on a journey to bigger and better things. Even me, a Liverpool 'thicko' (or so I thought at the time) felt like I belonged for the first time. Abraham Maslow's third hierarchy of needs says that we all feel the need to be involved in something special, so it was perhaps unsurprising that singing Beatles songs while standing in the Kop made me feel good about myself and feel like I belonged. Shankly used to say that the only real limitation on what you can accomplish is how badly you want something. I realise now that your own desire determines your destiny.

Outside of my Beatles and Liverpool FC mania, life continued much the same as it always had, but a little bit more positively because of my role models.

I became a qualified cabinet maker at Hygena, but I failed to become truly happy and lacked the insight as to why this was the case. Had I been better educated, I would have understood Maslow's theory, which states that the root of all happiness and fulfilment lies in self-actualisation. It is so important that you find work that fulfils, stretches and excites you, work that makes the music play inside of you.

The old saying that when God made us, he broke the mold, means that we are all unique with individual talents and skills. Although we are all similar physiologically speaking, we are truly our own people, put on this earth with an order to do something wonderful with our lives. I was unhappy simply because I had failed to identify my special skills and wasn't achieving my true potential in my role as a cabinet maker. Even though the pay was reasonable, and there was good comradeship at work, I still felt like I was in the wrong place, to the point that anger continually built up inside me. As soon as the hooter in the factory went off each night, I would run out of the door like a fire alarm had gone off. I was so unhappy but, worse still, I failed to leave my frustrations on the factory floor, instead taking them out on my parents and friends. Drinking became a popular pastime of mine, anything to escape the humdrum of my life. It is said that when you find a job you love; you will never work another day in your life. It's little wonder I had an almighty chip on my shoulder.

A Cry for Help

My actions were a cry for help, but, like millions of other people who hate their jobs, I failed to do anything about it. I didn't try to undertake additional education, nor did I train for a new role. Instead I unconsciously chose to stay in my comfort zone, blaming everyone else for my miserable life. I was like a revolving door, just standing there shouting and screaming for someone else to push the damn door and set me free. If only I had benefited from the understanding that the people who know more achieve more, I would have been able to stop myself from following a path I found disappointing. Instead, I remained at the factory, stuck in my fearful comfort zone before marrying at the age of 27, simply because that's what everyone else was doing. One good thing that did come (quickly) from my marriage was the birth of my beautiful daughter Joanne.

Her arrival made me desire a better home for my family but looking around at some of the older workers in the factory made me realise that if I didn't move my backside, I would end up just like them, wasting away with no real reason or purpose to my life. They were my colleagues, my comrades, and I had a good relationship with them, but it was becoming abundantly clear that I must not end up like them.

The working-class lads who had taken me under their wing when I left school at 14 ½ - Little Sam, Big Ernie, Harry the Horse, Lenny the Animal and Stinky the Tea Boy - were all in much the same boat. Self-actualisation was nothing more than a pipe dream, aside for those cabinet makers who had truly found their acres of diamonds doing what they were born to do. I had not found that same level of satisfaction in my life, so it was unsurprising that my brain was screaming at me to do more, imploring me to stop suppressing my feelings and staying in my comfort zone alongside my mates. I was becoming increasingly depressed, longing for a divine intervention to take away my discontent. It is perhaps a result of a miracle that I could take action when my opportunity finally arose and find my music inside. Peter Drucker said, "The very best way to predict your future is to create it yourself". My chance to create my own fortune was to present itself, and I would grab it with both hands.

Social Intelligence

I found that my level of social intelligence meant that I was good with people. There are, in fact, seven levels of social intelligence, and I scored highly on the social intelligence known as intra-personal intelligence. In short, people could relate to me and would respond accordingly. I realised that my mind needed to be nourished and that I no longer wished to forge a career as a cabinet maker, but I had no idea that the light at the end of my tunnel would arise after I was asked to become the manager of a football team that was set up at the factory. At first, I was clueless and useless in the role. Enthusiasm and motivation were not the problem, but rather that I had literally no idea what it took to be a successful manager - of anything! If we were to stop losing game after game, immediate action was required. I set about buying books about football management. The facts of management were suddenly laid out in front of me. I couldn't put this newfound knowledge down. The most memorable writing came from Manchester City's Malcolm Allison, and the most inspirational words, from Liverpool's Bill Shankly. Their words made me think that I could make a success of the Hygena football team, but it didn't take long for me to realise that the skills that I was learning were transferable. I hadn't read a book in years, likely since my school days, but my fascination with reading grew quickly.

The Hygena Football Team

I avidly soaked up information about 4-2-2 strategies and 4-3-3 formations and as my knowledge grew, so did the number of wins for the football team. We won cup after cup, building quite a name for the Hygena team. I even managed to convince the director to fork out for our own private pitch next to the Kirkby factory. The results the team was getting started to attract an even better quality of player from the Sunday leagues. Big Dan, Tommy 'Rocky' Hancock and Frankie Johnson 'The Wizard', whom I believe would have had a chance at playing in today's premier league teams, all joined the team, each time playing with heart and courage until the job was done, sometimes even bringing the score back from the brink to a win. Of course, it wasn't all smooth sailing. Some jibes from my rough and ready team and their weird sense of humour once incensed a manager from an opposing team to jump in his car and chase us around the pitch. We had to run for our lives but were at least able to laugh about it in the pub later.

My success as a football manager had a positive impact on my entire life. I felt on top of the world and no longer blamed the world for my perceived shortcomings. I stopped arguing with people and started to drink socially for enjoyment rather than to drown my sorrows. My confidence was growing with every goal, and I felt ready for change. Abe Lincoln said, 'I will study and prepare myself, and one day my chance will come.'

My own chance came because I was not the only person to realise my attitude had changed for the better. The managers at Hygena has also noticed the changes in me and invited me to take on a role as the company's social secretary. I gratefully accepted and, in doing so, became responsible for organising the social activities for a staff of 1,200. I took to it like a duck to water. It just came so naturally to me. I was experiencing Maslow's concept of self-actualisation as I organised multiple social activities for my colleagues and their families. My managers obviously felt the same, as it wasn't too long before they offered me yet another promotion; this time to that of the personnel manager for the factory. As you might imagine, I was shocked, pleased and out of my comfort zone all over again. It took the director of the company to convince me I was the right man for the job, telling me that my success as the social secretary and football manager proved I had the right skill set. Despite harbouring inner thoughts about my lack of training and experience for the role, I resolved to get on with the job. My bosses had confidence in me, so there was nothing to do but go for it.

The Pain of Failure
It was nine months later that the bombshell was dropped on

me. Having been called to see the directors, I was told that the Hygena factory was to close and all the workers were to be made redundant. My heart pounded, and tears filled my eyes, as I realised that the colleagues of which I had grown so fond were to lose their livelihood. What's worse is that it would be my job to tell them. After all I was the 'fake' personnel manager. The Thatcher government and the fighting Labour Party had been a veritable death knell for the people who lived and worked in Liverpool, but until that point, I still felt a little removed from the disastrous effect the Tory government was having on the city. But now, there was no escaping it. A factory that had employed people for more than 40 years was closing. I was in shock, so much so that, looking back, I realise that this was the first time in my life I had experienced the dark night of the soul. I also went through the five stages of grief; denial, anger, blame, depression and acceptance. To me, the decision was incomprehensible.

There had been no warning and no cutting back on shifts as a hint of what was to come. On the contrary, the factory was still running with 12-hour shifts, day and night. How could there be no work?

I was told I must inform the staff the next day. I was to give them 24 hours' notice and warn them that if there was any damage caused to the factory's equipment, the cost would be deducted from any redundancy payment. It didn't take me long to realise that this had all been planned. They had selected me months in advance to act as a sacrificial lamb. I had walked into what I thought was a promotion with my eyes firmly closed. That night was a sleepless one as I fretted about how to deliver such terrible news to my colleagues and friends.

It's All Over

The morning on which I was to make the dreaded announcement to the workforce saw all my colleagues summoned to the canteen. There was a hopeful mood in the air, likely because my workmates half expected to be told there was more overtime available. In a million years, they could never have foreseen the bombshell I was about to drop. Having been called to order by the Managing Director, who told them that, "Mr Haynes has an important announcement," my colleagues fell silent and looked at me expectantly. With something that resembled butterflies tearing away at my stomach, I tried to look as calm as I could but, as I began to speak, the sight of more than 1,000 hopeful faces caused my words to falter. I tried to compose myself as best I could, but I still stumbled over every word as I delivered the bad news, "I'm sorry, team. It's all over. We have been made redundant." I felt myself shaking like a leaf as it suddenly dawned on me that my rise from cabinet maker, to football manager, to social secretary and to personnel manager had all led up to this soul-destroying moment.

It was clear from the looks of my colleagues' faces that not a single member of the workforce had taken in what I had just said. Instead, my words were met with a roar of laughter and chants of 'Turn it in, Haynesey, how much overtime is there?' It was clear they thought the whole thing was nothing but a big wind up. I don't mind telling you that at this point, tears were starting to spill from my eyes, the sight of which made my colleagues start to look at one another in dawning disbelief. The truth was finally beginning to sink in. Envisaging trouble, the directors left the stage, leaving me to face the consequent uproar on my own. I repeated the news once again to my colleagues, also stating emphatically that if there were any trouble, redundancy money would not be forthcoming. A temporary lull that was so silent it was deafening fell over the room as my colleagues finally understood what was happening to them. I could almost see the beginnings of the five stages of death unfolding before my eyes: denial, anger, blame, depression, but would there be any acceptance?

My colleagues were facing the prospect of losing their jobs in an era when work was hard to come by in Liverpool. The questions of how they would feed their family, and pay their bills were obviously at the forefront of their minds as their emotions turned from denial to anger. Some of these people had worked at the factory for 40 years. In their minds, this was nothing short of a bereavement. Harry the Horse and Lenny the Animal took it worse of all, visibly breaking down in tears despite their usual tough-guy demeanour. Old Ernie carried on humming, but his hum took on an audible tone of sadness. Having been there for 18 years myself, having celebrated weddings, birthdays and the arrival of new babies and even funerals, I offered my condolences at times of sorrow, I felt the same way; only I was looked upon differently because I had been put in a position where I was the one forced to deliver the bad news. I resolved to use my new position as a positive force, to make sure my colleagues calmed down enough to ensure they would at least receive their redundancy pay.

The Beginning of the End

The day I delivered this awful news to the Hygena factory workers remains one of the worst days of my life. Not only did I feel so dreadfully sorry for the workmates I had grown up alongside, I felt angry with myself for allowing myself to be used as a puppet by those too spineless to deliver the news themselves. How had I not seen this coming? I resolved to keep my colleagues' spirits up as much as I could, trying my best to reassure everybody that we would all be able to find a new job and could remain friends. I managed to convince the directors to fork out for a leaving party, telling them in no uncertain terms that it was the very least they could do. There were tears and laughter in equal measure as we all clocked off together, walking shoulder to shoulder to the gates as we sang 'You'll never walk alone'.

Comrades in Arms

The leaving party took place in the Maghull Country Club, where office workers, shop floor guys and managers drank to old times, reminiscing about our time at the factory. We were all in it together as we hugged, laughed and raised a glass or two.

Afterwards, we went our separate ways, some going on to se-cure new jobs almost immediately, others never to work again. From time to time, news filtered in that one of the factory workers had died, some say because the abrupt change in their circumstances resulted in a broken heart that could never be mended. I, myself, remained in a state of shock for quite some time, on the brink of a nervous breakdown due to the stresses of the situation in which I had found myself. I had joined the dole queue and was haunted by a feeling of hopelessness and despair as stony-faced employment officers looked at me like I was something they had wiped off their shoe. I had, after all, left school at just 14½ and despite my various roles in the factory had no tangible qualifications to prove my worth. I was, indeed, worthless. A black cloud of despair filled with worry about my future and that of my family took up residence above my head.

As it happens, during any dark night of the soul, when times are at their hardest, and everything is black, a bright star will suddenly begin to shine like a beacon of light leading those affected out of a gloomy tunnel. This is exactly what was to happen to me, a bright star that came into my life and changed it completely, placing me firmly onto a new path toward the successful life I enjoy today. If you ever find yourself in a simi-lar situation, you'll know your bright star when you see it. You can't really miss it, but you must be prepared to act. I will intro-duce you to the man who changed my life in the next chapter but, for now, a reflection - so much time has gone by since my days at Hygena, I have been able to reflect on the situation only to realise that as traumatic as it was at the time, it served to make me a stronger and more determined person in the long run. Dire situations can always turn into learning curves, but it's up to you to remain strong and possess sufficient willpower to make it happen.

To my fine friends from Hygena, not least my beloved foot-ball team, I thank you all from the bottom of my heart. You saw me safely through the passage from boy to man. You offered me fun and friendship and a great deal of care and compassion along the way. You have been in my heart since those good old days and will remain so until the day my time on this earth is over. My memories of you all are among the best memories I have. Once again, thank you. I hope you are all flying with the eagles. I miss you all, Sad Sam Harry the Horse Humming Ernie, Lenny the Animal, and my world-beating football team. Some of them have died now. So, rest in peace, my true comrades, even as I write this, tears are flooding my eyes. I love you all. Good-bye Hygena - I hope you are all flying with the eagles and not scratching with the turkeys

Test your memory and put this knowledge into your long-term memory.

1. What was the name of the factory where I worked and how many years did I work there?
2. What was the name of the factory foreman?
3. What did everybody do on the bus going home?
4. Which Beatles song did I sing at the Kop?
5. As an Everton fan, which manager did I idolise?
6. What hours did I work every day?
7. Which political parties went to war with each other, resulting in the loss of thousands of jobs?
8. Where was the Hygena factory situated?
9. What were the names of some of my former workmates at the factory?
10. What were the positions I held at the Hygena factory?

The Principal of Affirmation says that strong, affirmation statements repeated continually in your conscious mind will inevitably be accepted as commands by your subconscious mind. Good luck.

2. I JUMPED INTO THE VALLEY OF BLAME

'Your mind is the most important and precious asset. You must protect it and keep it clean, clear and focused on what you want, rather than allowing it to be polluted by the negative influences around you.' Brian Tracy.

Learning from My Lost Time in the Wilderness

Thinking back to when I was 13/14, I remember my English teacher, Mr Forshaw, trying his best to impress on me what a fool I was being. As usual, I wasn't paying attention in class, choosing to daydream instead. He told me that the reason people can't find jobs and are being laid off is that they lack the necessary skills and knowledge. He felt that the way I was going, I was heading to the dole queue, telling me that the future belongs to those people with the ability to get results for their boss and those who are adding to their knowledge base every day. Mr Forshaw was so determined to make me understand what he was saying that he made me write it down. The words were undoubtedly profound, but they were wasted on me. As was the case with many words of wisdom imparted to me back then, they simply went over my head.

23 Years Later

There's an old saying that the rich get richer while the poor get poorer. I think it is better explained by saying that the rich get richer by gaining knowledge while the poor feel that education is for the boring and stuffy-nosed types. I was certainly getting poorer. Having left school at 14½, I hadn't even passed any exams.

I thought I knew it all but failed to realise that feedback is the breakfast of champions. I just concentrated on what was fun and easy and ignored anything that would benefit me in the longer term. I only I had understood that I was prioritising the short-term gain over the long-term pain and, in doing so, was condemning myself to long-term pain. Years later, that pain was to materialise in the worry of how I would feed my family and how I would pay the mortgage and indeed all the other bills that mounted up continually. I didn't realise that it had been the short-term gain I had enjoyed earlier that had led me to this long-term pain. In fact, it took me quite some years to realise the damage I had done by prioritising watching the TV instead of reading books to further my knowledge, by socialising in pubs instead of going to night school, and by going to endless football matches instead of spending quality time with my family.

Looking at it now, I deserved the pain of the dole queue and being worried sick about my bills. My short-term gain really didn't seem all that wonderful as my previous actions came to its inevitable conclusion. The words of the employment officer still ring in my ears to this day – 'Mr Haynes, in these hard times, you must realise that if you want to earn more, you must first learn more. Now go join the back of the queue.'

And believe me, in Liverpool, that queue was half a mile long. It was easy to fall into the mistake of blaming others. At the age of 33 I quickly joined my fellow 'dolites,' my new brothers and sisters, in laying the blame for our predicament at the door of our bosses, the government and the schools. I even blamed my parents. After all, they had brought me into this world. Of course, I knew deep down that it was my fault. If only I had taken the words of Mr Forshaw seriously.

Age 33, and Down and Out

We are all where we are today because of the decisions we have made in the past. I had decided to enjoy short-term thrills with no thought of the future. It was a decision that had led me to the dole queue, forced to continually encounter a look of shock on the employment officer's face as they realised I had left school at 14½ and had not undergone any sort of education or training since. It was the worst time ever in Liverpool to find work and be on the dole. The city was entering the age of the Boys of the Black Stuff, Alan Bleasdale's 1982 drama where Bernard Hill's character of Jimmy 'Yosser' Hughes uttered the now-famous phrase 'Gis a job'. Margaret Thatcher's Tory government was going head to head with Derek Hatton's Labour council. They hated each other. He countered strategies by calling seemingly endless strikes, a move which she responded to by refusing to invest in Liverpool. The normal folks were stuck in the middle.

The trust between the Tory government and Liverpool's Labour councillor was zero, and we were just pawns in the middle. I remember reading a book by the American political scientist, economist and author, Francis Fukuyama. 'Trust' looked at the varying levels of trust that existed in different nations. Fukuyama concluded that in high-trust nations, governments are more prosperous and offer greater opportunities to their people. There are more jobs, longer-term employment and greater security. Low-trust nations, on the other hand, suffer from lower employment levels, insecure futures for citizens, and less outside investment. The latter is of relevance to Liverpool. The Tory government sought to condemn Liverpool by withholding investment, choosing instead to force the city into decline. It was the everyday people who withstood the worst effects of this decision. Almost everything that fails can ultimately be attributed to a lack of trust.

Out of Denial

Me? I just carried on standing in that dole queue listening to the politicians, the so-called educated people, behaving like spoiled brats. I remember going home one night, after yet another fruitless day of looking for work, and looking at my (by then) sick wife and my young daughter Joanne and realising I had totally let them down. In that instant, I came out of my state of denial and saw the world how it was and not how I wished it to be. Despite the problems caused by the Tory-La-bour fighting, my situation was down to me alone. It was me who couldn't be bothered to educate myself. If only I had done things differently, I would not be standing in front of my family with tears of frustration rolling down my face. Joanne, of course, didn't understand why I was crying, so simply started crying herself. That moment was possibly the lowest point of my miserable life. I am sure that the Boys from the Black Stuff had similar experiences. We were all in the same boat. The only people who were on a steady wage in those days were the bloody politicians. Like thousands of other people, I was worried sick about my future. My mortgage payments were six months overdue, and my dark night of the soul continued to darken.

Negative Imagination

Psychologists now say that worry is simply a sustained fear caused by doubt and indecision. Worry is defined as a negative imagination or, in my case, negative goal setting. My thoughts were constantly on the things I didn't want to experience in my life, but I found that the more I complained, blamed and worried, the more of the same I encountered. You've no doubt heard of the Law of Attraction. This was exactly what I was experiencing. Whatever I thought about or talked about, which was usually negative, the more negativity that came into my life. When I worried, I simply attracted more worry into my life. I was my own worst enemy. I should have spent my time thinking about the things I wanted in my life. But no, I wasted time thinking about the things I didn't want. I had used the Law of Attraction to create my very own negative future.

German Bombs

I even worried about letting my parents down. I was, after all, the recipient of many handouts as they bailed me out with cash and paid some of my bills. My mother, Violet, used to tell me stories about her own life that made me realise that what I was going through really didn't compare. My mother and father, Jack, had lived through two world wars. In the second, my father had been sent overseas to fight for almost four years. Can you imagine being away from your family during such a terrifying time? My mother spoke of the terror she felt whenever the air raid sirens went off as another German bomber rained down their weapons of mass destruction on the streets of Liverpool. She didn't always make it to the shelter; instead she was forced to hide under the stairs, left to clutch my older brother and sister, Jimmy and Margaret, while she prayed to God to protect them from the devastation.

The bombs came so frequently that my poor mother's nerves were gone. My father was, of course, also fighting for his life, while having to listen to the stories that filtered through about his hometown being bombed and people dying on an almost nightly basis. My mother was right when she said that what she had gone through was surely not as bad as what had happened in those dark days of the war. Indeed, I was the wimp crying and moaning about having no work. It paled into comparison to what my parents had endured.

There is a lighter side to it all, of course, when Stan Boardman, the famous Liverpool comedian, coined the phrase 'The Germans bombed our chippy'. What I admire most, though, was how in those dark days, there was a sense that nobody was alone. Family, friends and neighbours all used to help one another out by sharing clothes and food. What a great feeling that must have been – a true sense of what's mine is yours. My mum used to tell me that I had to find the courage to survive. If she could do it in such a tough time, then I must surely be able to find the courage to get through my own problems.

Courage

Years later, when I was studying courage in greater depth, I came across a quote by Ralph Waldo Emerson – 'Do the thing you fear, and the death of fear is certain' and another saying that I feel especially applied to me. The saying explained the difference between a brave person and a coward, stating that a brave person is one who acts despite their fears. My parents were brave. I was just a coward with negative feelings and sorry-for-myself attitude. Mark Twain said that 'courage is resistance to fear, mastery of fear, not absence of fear.' My parents and the rest of their generation showed the fine qualities of courage while my generation – the Boys of the Black Stuff – did not. We were filled with anger and blame, and we lacked the conviction and resolve to get up and fight. One of my regrets in life is not telling my parents how much I loved and respected them before they died. I concentrated, instead, on telling them how awful my life was. If you are lucky enough to be able to say that your parents are still alive, please take the time to tell them how much you love them. That precious window will soon pass.

The Dole Queue

So, after I was made redundant from Hygena, I felt like I was a complete thicko. I had no job, no education to speak of and no money, much less a fortune. I felt angry, betrayed, and let down. The world, or more specifically, my world, was shit. As my time in the dole queue grew, so did my level of depression. It was my poor family who bore the brunt of my despair as I continued to moan at everyone about the living hell that had become my life. I had somehow concluded that the world owed me a living and, as a result, was a resident in the Valley of Blame.

Unbeknown to me, my life was soon to change. After waiting in the dole queue for another soul-destroying two hours, the employment officer greeted me with the words, "I think I might have found you a job." I felt my heart start to pound immediately as a feeling of excitement washed over me. In those seconds that followed, I allowed my mind to run riot. Would there be a company car involved? A great salary? Big bonuses? A great pension? Lots of holidays? My excitement soon turned to disappointment when I realised my big break was a commission-only gig for the Co-operative Insurance Society. I was to sell life insurance. And, if I failed to do so, there would be no pay packet at the end of the week.

Knocking Door to Door

Along with selling new life insurance policies (the hardest sell ever!), it would also be my responsibility to collect weekly premiums for existing policies. I was to work door to door in Bootle, one of the poorest and roughest areas of Liverpool. This area was renowned for its high unemployment levels and extreme poverty. In short, these people were even worse off than me. Ignoring the feeling of my heart sinking to my boots, I agreed to attend the interview regardless. Something was better than nothing, right?

The interview went ahead, and it soon became clear that a fair number of people who had been interviewed before me had been so put off by the prospect of door to door selling in one of the city's most downtrodden areas that they had refused the position. I, on the other hand, said yes. I think this amazed even the interviewer. Despite the glaringly obviously drawbacks to the position, I was worrying so much about my family, about losing my home and about what other people were saying behind my back that I really had no other choice. Accepting the position not only meant that I could finally tell my family that I had a job but also that I could avoid the indignity of the dole queue.

To be successful in my new position, I had to sell. There was no way around it and no dole money to act as a comfort blanket. It was up to me to grasp this opportunity with both hands and prove I could do this job well enough for it to put food on my family's table, catch up with my mortgage and hire purchase payments and clothe my daughter in a uniform that wouldn't cause her school friends to tease her. After spending two days training, I was hungry for success and ready to hit the streets. And hit them I did. As it turned out, the good people of Bootle had other ideas. Boy, was I in for a rude awakening?

Soul Destroying

In the first few weeks of the job, I lost count of the number of doors I had slammed in my face. The sound of those slamming doors, which was typically accompanied by a few choice words that I won't repeat here, was endless. It was painful and about as soul-destroying as the dole queue. The Co-op motto was that if you don't sell, you don't eat, and I sure did come close to that. Selling very little meant that I earned very little. My commission was pitiful and certainly a long way from an acceptable income for a man with a family to take care of. Despite the overwhelming feelings of rejection, degradation and failure that washed over me every time a door was slammed unceremoniously in my face, I resolved to keep going. After all, what was my alternative? I allowed myself to be spurred on by the words of a fellow but more successful salesman than me - *Some will, some won't, so what next?* I repeated these words to myself after each rejection and forcing myself to plaster a smile on my face; I continued to knock on those doors.

Persistence

Gradually, the slammed doors started to be replaced by a willingness to listen. Looking back, I think the people in that deprived area of Liverpool began to see me as one of their own, and slowly but surely, they began to buy policies from me. I remember the first week that I could legitimately call myself successful. I only sold three policies but, at the time, the feeling of euphoria these sales gave me meant everything. I could finally start to see a glimpse of light at the end of, what had been, a very long tunnel. I was going to make it. I still didn't really have a clue what I was doing but, as it turned out, it didn't matter. The people were buying into me rather than a life insurance policy. That week taught me that people do have hearts and do want to help others. My humility and persistence had begun to pay off, and every time a woman said something like, "Oh, go on then.

I'll take a policy. At least if the husband goes, I'll be able to bury him and have a few drinks in his name," it felt like birdsong in my heart. I was finally making something of my life.

In time, I sold more policies and even started to collect on some overdue premiums. Things were going well, and I felt an almost constant sense of achievement as I knocked on door after door before heading home on my little bike - a bike I had bought to get me around the streets and home to my family quicker. That bike became my trademark but ultimately would become my downfall. My bike became a constant sight on the streets of Bootle. Everyone knew it belonged to the Co-op man. Unfortunately, everyone included a gang of local thugs who had begun to realise that the guy on the trademark bike carried a satchel with money in it. My new-found heaven turned to hell when that gang of thugs came for me. I was done for the night and about to head home when they jumped me. It was all over in a matter of minutes, but a matter of minutes was all it took to steal my money, break my bike, and leave me bleeding on the ground.

A Broken Man

I stumbled home a broken man who could barely look his sick wife and young daughter in the eyes. I'm not ashamed to admit I cried that night. Angry tears born out of frustration and desperation slid down my cheeks as I realised that once again, I had failed. In times of crisis, it is often said that things will look better in the morning. That didn't prove to be the case for me. The Co-op, having heard about what had happened, made it abundantly clear that I was responsible for the lost money, and would need to replace it out of my own pocket. Should I fail to do so, they would involve the police. Not only would I be a failure, I would also be a criminal. It is probably not very surprising that my new feelings of hope and achievement were immediately replaced by the earlier thought patterns that had so skilfully assured me that I was a worthless human being.

Dark Night of the Soul

As it was, after 35 years of being on this earth and some 20 years since I had left school, I was in a crisis. Things were getting worse, not better. I had no education. I was in a job that nobody else wanted. I couldn't support my family. Even my trusty little bike had been dragged into my mess. After the robbery, I was left with no choice but to ask my parents for help. God bless them. Even though they had so little themselves, they agreed to help me out with a handout. I felt awful taking money from them but being able to put food on my family's table did bring some light relief.

Despite the financial help afforded by my parents, I really was going through the dark night of the soul. Most people experience this desperation at some point in their lives. For me, it came in the form of awakening around 3 am, each morning, in a cold sweat and with a sense of dread about my worries and problems. At that time in life, I felt like I was the loneliest person in the world. Experts say that the only way to be successful is not to quit so, despite seeing no hope for my future, I hung on in there. I agreed to pay back the stolen money to the Co-op in instalments. It was an agreement that was to save my position at the company and prevent the police from coming to my door. Of course, it also meant that my family had even less to live on and my borrowing increased. The loan sharks who were out in force in Liverpool at the time were having a field day with me.

My Bright Star

It was not long after I began to drag myself back to my feet that a miracle happened. After all, it is when the sky is at its darkest, that the brightest stars shine. My miracle came in the form of a one-day sales and motivation course laid on by the Co-op. Every salesperson in the company was ordered to attend, including me. Having thought that my education had ended when I had left school at the tender age of 14½, I was somewhat nervous about entering a classroom again. But nonetheless, I duly attended although my lack of self-confidence, thanks to my inability to fill out a form neatly, to write a legible letter and to even look a person in the eye, meant that I headed straight for a seat at the back. I mean, God forbid should I be in the firing line for any questions.

To my surprise, I found the course fascinating. The trainer, a business professor from a local college, had a vast amount of experience in the fields of sales and motivation and, as the day went on, I felt myself becoming increasingly inspired by what this guy was saying. I was literally hanging onto his every word and was disappointed when the clock signified the end of the day. If I had still been at Hygena, I would have run from the door at shutting up time as if a fire had begun to take over the building. I witnessed that same attitude in my colleagues that day. When the training ended, they all just got up and left. There were no words of thanks, no round of applause, just a mass exodus from the room. I was the last man standing, and I was nothing short of embarrassed by the rude behaviour of my colleagues. Without looking the presenter in the eye, I plucked up the courage to apologise for their rudeness and to say that I had enjoyed his presentation.

The 80/20 Rule of Listening

The saviour thanked me for my kind words and, unexpectedly, asked me what I was doing working for a hardnosed and uncaring company in such a rough area of Liverpool. I tentatively explained that my shortcomings including my lack of education combined with the need to provide for my family meant that jobs were hard to come by. The gig for the Co-op, although by no means anything to shout about from the rooftop, was at least a job and something I could take a small sense of pride in, and it helped me avoid thinking too much about the realities of my life. The presenter stared at me intensely and, at that moment, I realised that he was listening to me. I felt compelled to continue and blurted out all about my failings - my family worries, my money problems, and the shame I felt at borrowing money from my elderly parents and about having been beaten up by what was likely no more than a gang of teenagers. And guess what? This guy continued to listen to me.

I have since learned that listening is one of the top skills in life. It's called 'white magic' and he was using it on me. By listening so intently about 80 per cent of the time and using the remaining 20 per cent of the time to ask searching questions, he had made me feel important. For the first time in my life, I felt like someone who was worth listening to. Intense listening is the greatest form of flattery. We all have our fears, worries and a sense of loneliness at times but when people take the time to actively listen to our concerns without feeling the need to interrupt unnecessarily, those doubts and fears can dissipate in that given time. All the while, I was unloading my concerns on the speaker, I was wondering how an intelligent and clever man such as him could possibly be interested in what I had to say, much less even have the time to spend with a low-level person such as myself. I also learned later that his skills were a strong indicator of his leadership abilities. Wordsworth said that the only way to judge the character of a person, is to look at the way they treat people who are in some way in a lesser position than themselves. You can get a sense of a person's true value as a leader in this way. The speaker had proved himself to be a strong leader.

It was likely sheer desperation that led me to go on to ask this mentor for help that day. I wasn't after his money. I just sought his knowledge and his help to make me feel more confident and worthwhile as a person. Finally finding the courage to ask for someone's help rather than their money meant that I had inadvertently stumbled on a lucky day, as that professor was to prove to be the brightest star in my darkest of nights. He told me that he would be around these parts for three months and suggested that we should meet in a local cafe for an hour every Tuesday morning. At the same time, he warned me that should I ever be late or fail to act on his advice, that would be the end of our meetings, and I would have to go it alone. He also requested that I furnish him with a coffee and a bacon butty each time we met. Fighting back feelings of complete and utter shock at the realisation that this inspirational guy had just agreed to help me, I stumbled out some form of acceptance to his demands. It was incredible to think that someone was willing to help me to escape from the nightmare I was living. That's the beauty of the world. People will often go out of their way to make a difference in other people's lives. I think people that have learned this skill have learned from role models, like the caring Mother Teresa of Calcutta. Trying not to think about how I would afford to buy this guy breakfast the following Tuesday, I bid my new-found saviour goodbye and set off home to repair my little bike and tell my daughter that good things were finally on the way for us all.

The very next Tuesday, I met with the professor in Big Sally's Café. As I feared a week earlier, I lacked the funds to supply him with his requested bacon butty, so I bluffed it out and simply pretended to myself that he didn't really want one. The cafe was clean but small but, as it happens, that matters not. The mind can learn anywhere should it choose to do so. It's a good job too because my new-found friend wasted no time at all in starting to teach me his three golden secrets for success. While I chose not to tell him that I didn't understand what he meant when he used the words visual, kinaesthetic, and auditory, his claim that the knowledge he was about to teach me would change my life has stayed with me forever.

Leaders are Readers

When the professor asked me if I read books, I was so embarrassed to have to tell him that I wasn't all that into reading. He told me that leaders are readers and if I wanted to be successful then I was going to have to make a change. To help me to do that, he wanted to know why I wasn't so keen on reading books. I explained that every time I tried to read a book, I would get to the bottom of each page and realise that I couldn't remember what

I had just read much less understand it. As a result, I became disillusioned and bored with the whole process. He didn't make me feel stupid when I said this but rather said I was in a similar situation to a lot of people and that, maybe if he had the time, he would include lessons in power and speed reading in our lessons. His initial advice, though, was that I was simply reading the wrong books. From that point forward, I should only buy books that addressed my problems. Given that my problems were both numerous and diverse, I told him that his advice had left a fairly large number of possible books to be added to my bookshelf.

Nonetheless, he persisted with his advice that I should buy books that would help me to earn more money in my job, to improve my confidence and to help me to become a better salesman. He told me that by buying books of real interest to me would mean that I wouldn't get bored. I would subconsciously use both sides of my brain. The emotional right side of my brain would get involved, and the left-hand analytical side would combine the words to the right pictures in the right-hand side of the brain.

Of course, I followed his advice. I had no choice but to do so. It felt that the hand of God had reached down to lift me up and out of a life of misery and despair. The professor had come into my life just before I went into a total meltdown and quite probably a long-term depression. As the weeks went by, I came to understand what Paul Getty meant when he said that if you wanted to help the poor, you should avoid becoming one of them. What I didn't quite grasp was that my saviour was using his superior knowledge to help me, so, in turn, I would later be able to help people who were less fortunate than myself.

Life-Changing

My mentor went on to elaborate on how reading could improve my life, instructing me that I should read for one hour each day. At the thought of devoting an hour of each day of my life to books, it seemed that a look of panic crossed my face. He must have noticed this fleeting look of despair as he relented and made the alternative suggestion that I read for half an hour in the morning and for half an hour in the evening. By doing so, not only would I get through a book each week, I would consume an average of four books each month and 50 books each year. The thought of this made my head spin but, undeterred, my mentor explained that all the knowledge that would soon be mine would help drag me from the bottom of the ladder, or where I was now, to the very top of my chosen career. All I would need is the discipline and willpower to get it done. Almost to cement my decision to take on his reading challenge, he pointed out that if I didn't love my family enough and wanted to keep on with the self-pity and woe is me attitude, I should simply not do it. Presumably, had I taken this route; our meetings would also have ended. According to my mentor, everybody wants the nice things in life, but nobody wants to pay the price. He asked me whether I was someone who was unwilling to pay the price, or would I commit to reading for just one hour each day, finishing off with a rather sarcastic, "Your choice, scouser."

Neural Grooves

It became clear that this guy was serious, so yes, I had better pay the price and commit to learning through reading. I felt like I had made the right choice when he explained that everything we do in life is a habit. A habit can be good or bad, but it is a habit nonetheless and that, once established in the mind, it is there to stay; thanks to the formation of a new brain pathway (known as a neural groove) being formed. If I could only start building new pathways, it was likely that in ten years' time I would have absorbed the knowledge of 500 books. This fact alone, would help propel me into the top five per cent of any profession I chose to follow. I must admit that I struggled to take this all in. I mean, how could I, a person with limited education and a distinct lack of belief in myself, ever be classed as being in the top five per cent of anything? My mentor put my fears somewhat to bed when he stated that if I was to come to believe in myself and my abilities with feeling and emotion, then good things would come into my reality. Being the outspoken person that he was, he also told me to just bloody well start believing in myself and get on with the climb to the top five per cent. Regardless of my inner doubts, the whole thing was music to my ears. My heart was pounding as I imagined myself as a successful person in the future.

My mentor didn't mention the lack of a bacon butty on the first week we met, but I was not so lucky the second time around when he asked where his breakfast was. Thinking on my feet, and all too conscious of the fact that I simply didn't have the funds to buy him a butty, I blamed Big Sally for forgetting our order. It's a good job she couldn't hear what we were saying; Big Sally was not known for a calm demeanour and understanding attitude. On the contrary, as I looked over at the woman herself, she pointed two fingers to her eyes and then pointed them straight at me, as if to say watch it because I'm sure as hell watching you. Gulp!

Moving on from his earlier suggestion that I should up the amount I was reading, my mentor suggested that I should play Baroque music in the background while reading. This would apparently help both sides of my brain to relax, and for the knowledge I was taking in to flow from the left-hand side of the brain to the right where the long-term memory resides. Upon asking him where I would find this special music, he told me that I should use my mind and find it for myself. Knowing nothing about music, I asked again as we left the cafe while choosing to ignore the sound of Big Sally's fist crashing on the table in frustration at not having gotten a breakfast order from us. He told me well it's certainly not from a pub so why not try a music store that sells classical music? And that I did. I was, at last, starting to take responsibility for my own future.

The following week, I arrived early at the cafe, hoping my mentor would arrive and had not yet given up on me. He hadn't and was there waiting for me. He asked straight out whether I had bought a self-improvement book, read for half an hour in the morning and half an hour in the night and played and listened to Baroque music while I was reading. I was thrilled to be able to gleefully answer yes, yes, yes to all the questions, but my positive response was not enough. This guy wanted proof, and I was happy to oblige, ignoring the fact that I was scared that I had not done enough and, as a result, he would simply abandon me, leaving me back at square one and back in my life of hell and hopelessness. This man had offered me the hand of friendship, and I didn't want to let him down, especially since I had felt able to tell my parents that I had found someone who believed in me and had high expectations of me. As Aristotle once said, "It's not what you want in life; it's what you expect." I had up until then expected bad things to happen to me and I wasn't far wrong, but the professor's expectations of me meant that I was starting to expect better things for myself.

I showed the professor the books I had chosen, one on sales and one on self-confidence. I could assure him that he had been so right with his advice. Despite only being instructed to read for half an hour each morning and evening, I had felt unable to put the books down. It was if they had been written for me and were already making me feel better about myself. giving me hope and confidence. As he examined the books, he asked me what all the stamp marks were. I went bright red with embarrassment as I explained that I had mistakenly taken them from the library but planned to return them and pay the fees as soon as I had earned enough. For the record, I did exactly that one year later but, at the time, my mentor rolled his eyes in shock, shook his head, and muttered something about bloody scousers. Of course, Big Sally was by now circling the table in the expectation of getting an order. I simply spoke louder to drown out her voice because I still didn't have enough money to pay for his bloody bacon butty.

Despite the lack of a bacon sandwich in front of him, I think he could see I think that I wasn't a lost cause and that I had set my mind on self-improvement. Therefore, he continued to offer advice. From that point forward, I was to continue with my reading to music habit, but I was also to start disfiguring the book as I read it. I really didn't understand what the professor meant but didn't have the confidence to question why I should disfigure the book. Who was I to argue? A command had been given, and I was compelled to follow that command. I resolved to disfigure my books page by page, still not really understanding why and how I would achieve this new instruction.

The following Tuesday soon arrived and, as usual, I was relieved that I was not the only one to turn up, not least because I finally had enough cash on me to shout for breakfast. He, of course, was more interested in asking me to elaborate on the actions I had taken the week before. I nervously explained that I had kept up with the reading, but as I hadn't been too sure what he meant about disfiguring the books as I did so, I had simply resorted to scribbling on each page before ripping it out of the book. After a somewhat stunned silence, my mentor slammed his fist on the table while yelling that he hadn't meant to do that. This unexpected action led to Big Sally looking about ready to give us a Glasgow kiss, so I figured it would be a good time to finally throw in an order for bacon butties for two. Perhaps it was the thought that he would finally get to eat a spot of breakfast that softened the response from my mentor but, either way, he admitted that he perhaps hadn't been as clear as he could have been.

Thankfully, he decided to explain what he had meant. From that point on, when I was reading, I should always have a highlighter pen with me to highlight the text in colour, but only the parts I had encountered difficulty understanding and the parts that I found interesting and of importance. Since the brain is stimulated by colour, I was to use different colours to denote different things. When going back to the text, I would be able to pick out the highlighted areas to refine my thoughts and could easily locate the salient points to make connections within my brain. Reviewing the books, you read is just as important as the actual reading, but the use of colour to highlight facts and interesting quotes made it easier for the brain to commit knowledge to the long-term memory. Passages of text I understood the first time around, I could simply add a tick to lock in what I had learned. The only thing my mentor was perhaps still unsure of was how I would explain the missing pages to the librarian.

Be on Time

The following week, with my mentor's words of wisdom ringing in my ears, I arrived at the cafe a full half-hour early. I had even managed to scrape together enough money for another round of bacon butties although, in all honesty, that was probably due to a fear of upsetting Big Sally as opposed to any real desire to spring for breakfast. My mentor arrived, as he usually did, on time. By doing so, I felt that he was showing me how important it is to be disciplined regarding time management. To that end, he never once missed a session, nor was he ever late or failed to finish on time.

Although I perhaps didn't realise it at the time, this consistent behaviour was having a big impression on me and was to prove to be a solid grounding for when I ran meetings in a large insurance company years later. I later learned that once a habit is formed, whether good or bad, it can stay with you forever. I also learned that what the professor was doing was using the Law of Suggestology during the time we spent together. This law advocates that up to 90 per cent of what we do is a result of outside influences. It is perhaps more easily understood when you consider how you feel after spending the day hearing depressing news and spending time with negative people. We don't feel great, right? On the flip side, if you avoid the news and actively surround yourself with positive thinkers, we feel a whole lot better as a result.

My Sin

My mentor took his seat, all the while on the receiving end of the evil eye of Big Sally. Having glanced at her just momentarily, he asked "Are all Liverpool women like this?" I quipped back,

"No, Big Sally is one of the nicest people you'll ever meet - just wait until you meet a nasty girl."

Having cast his eyes to the ceiling in mock despair, he advised that we get our order in before we were both jettisoned out of the window. Order placed, and the big lady herself appeased for at least a little while, he got straight down to the business of putting my feet to the fire, asking me sternly if I had borrowed a book from the library and read it for the required hour each day. He further questioned whether I had listened to the prescribed Baroque music while reading, and if I had disfigured the book with highlighter pens as I read. I was pleased to pass this impromptu test with flying colours. Never in my life had I scored 100 per cent on anything, so it was something of a milestone for me. Feeling like a winner, I added coffee to our order of bacon butties.

The professor was not only educating me but was also building my shattered self-confidence and self-esteem. It's one of the reasons why I now strongly believe that everyone who wants to succeed in life should have a personal mentor. After all, sporting champions have their own mentors, so it follows that those in business should have one too. With his coffee and bacon butty now in front of him, my mentor's next question was to ask whether I had a car. Now as it happened, a sympathetic friend had just given me an old banger. It was nice of him, but that car really was a wreck, so much so that I had parked it around the corner for fear of my mentor seeing it. It didn't even have any tax on it, never mind a valid MOT. Despite my embarrassment, I took a big gulp and told him that, yes, I did have a car. I didn't mention that my trusty old bike was safely stored in the boot. I had considered getting rid of it, but we had been through so much together that I couldn't bear to part with. Plus, I was a lot more streetwise than I once was, always on the lookout for greedy gangs and, if I'm truly honest, feeling a lot safer simply for making an acquaintance of the fearsome Big Sally.

Bubble Gum Music

He then asked me whether my car had a tape player in it or just a radio. I informed him that, yes, the car did have a little stereo, but I only ever listened to the radio. Another look of despair flashed across his face as he explained that I was listening to bubble gum music. On seeing the puzzled look on my face, he continued to explain that listening to the music that is played on the radio is rather like putting bubble gum in your brain. The constant thump, what he termed boom, boom, confuses the brain, making it sticky. When you eventually switch off the radio and get out of the car, your brain is closed and wobbly. The impact of this music on your brain is so strong that it can cause you to act in a strange way, to not think clearly and to generally underperform in life. The brain is effectively terrorised by the music. With that in mind, it came as little surprise that his next statement was to say that if I was to remain a student of his, I must stop immediately. This I did.

If You're Not Getting Better, You're Getting Worse

I was learning that everything counts. Either you are reading, acting on your increased knowledge, spending time with positive people and moving forward in the direction of your goal or you're hanging out with negative people, watching TV for hours on end each evening, listening to bubble gum music and moving backwards and away from your dreams. There are no half measures. Either you're doing it all, or you're not doing anything. It was then that he uttered the words that were to momentarily leave me dumbfounded. He told me that I was to turn my car into a university on wheels. While not fully understanding what he meant, I quietly responded that I hadn't even made it to college let alone university. Smiling wryly, he told me that my subconscious brain could learn anywhere, going on to say that a classroom situation was not necessary. All that was needed for the brain to absorb new knowledge was a place that I wasn't likely to feel stressed. According to my mentor some of the most educated people in the world had learned behind the steering wheel while driving. I found this concept difficult to understand at first and, going by the look of confusion cast by Big Sally from the back of the cafe, so did she. Unperturbed, he described how playing tapes from experts while driving makes that driving time learning time. The university of life experts had put all their knowledge and skills into one little cassette. All I had to do was listen. After all, why would I go through life trying to reinvent the wheel when I could learn from people who had already made the mistakes and come through them to be successful. "You can do this, John, and you can do it in your car." he said.

"Not if the police catch him for having no tax, he can't," added Big Sally.

Uni On Wheels

I was by now used to being completely thrown by pretty much everything that came from my mentor's mouth but it still didn't stop me from looking at him in amazement when his next question was whether I would be willing to attend a 200-hour seminar where I would have access to the best tutors and gurus in the world. My attendance would turn me into a centre of excellence, would get me better jobs and would give me financial freedom. With my mind running riot with pictures of holidays and houses and even images of me paying for my own round in the pub, I still found my self-limiting beliefs coming into play as I told him I wouldn't have time nor could I afford access to such knowledgeable people. A slight laugh escaped his lips as he explained that all I would have to do to attend such a seminar is to listen to tapes in the car. The average person drives for an astonishing 200 hours every year. If they were to just listen to tapes while they drove, it would be the equivalent of attending 200 hours of seminars each year.

On top of that, he explained, I wouldn't have to be a wimp, panic, squirm or make excuses. All I needed to do was play the damn tape. This would enable me to learn any skill I desired.

Perhaps I would like to learn the art of time management or how to be a better salesman. Maybe I would like to learn a foreign language. "In short, John, driving time is learning time. Don't you dare waste another minute listening to the news or bubble gum music while driving. Make your car a university on wheels and start living in the educational world."

And from that day, that's exactly what I have done. Nowadays, I can't get in the car without listening to the words of an expert. Of course, the words flow from my iPhone these days, but the principle is the same. What I have learned over the years that have followed is that the professor was right. I have learned more, and I have certainly earned more as a result. I have passed on this advice to many people, although one springs to mind. A friend who wanted to learn corporate accountancy was driving between Liverpool and London regularly for work and, on my advice, started to use this time to listen to audio teaching. It took him two years to pass his exams, never having set foot in a classroom. He and I are just two of no doubt millions of people who have learned in this fashion. What's stopping you from doing the same?

In the meantime, of course, my face had dropped like a turkey's bum at the realisation of all the time I had wasted listening to bubble gum music while driving, when I could have been educating myself and then earning much-needed money for my family. What a plonker I had been. At last, I felt that the penny had dropped, and I was at last in control of my destiny. It felt rather like I had received a gift from God, a treasured gift that was to change my life. My mentor assured me that this was the case but that it was important that I use the knowledge that I learned. I should not become what he termed an educated derelict. There are some people who read books, listen to the tapes, and even go on numerous courses. What they don't do is anything with the knowledge they have learned. They think it is sufficient to walk the walk without talking the talk. They procrastinate and wonder why people still gossip behind their backs. Despite their efforts, they achieve nothing due to a lack of proper discipline. My mentor explained that these people do not have the true desire to grab their opportunity nor the commitment to achieve their goals.

I suddenly felt like I was in control of my own destiny. If it was to be, it was up to me, and I had the knowledge I needed to make a huge change in my life. The desire had always been present. Instead of being excited about having enough money to go to a football match or buy a pint in the pub, I now had the belief that I could change my future. I had unexpectedly been released from my feelings of inadequacy and chains of self-doubt. These comforting thoughts were interrupted by the sound of Big Sally's fist slamming the fist of another customer down on a nearby table. The foolish sod had forgotten his money and had come up with the not-so-wise plan to challenge Big Sally to an arm wrestle in lieu of payment. Perhaps needless to say, she had taken him down in a matter of moments, at the same time shouting at him that he owed her double next time round.

My New Life

I worked harder than ever before to scrape together as much money as I could to spend on educational tapes that inspired me. I remember the first one I bought was the work of Zig Ziglar, an American author, salesman and motivational speaker. It was from that tape that I learned the significance of the saying, 'Fly with the eagles, don't scratch with the turkeys.' I made my car my own personal university on wheels and, to my surprise, Big Sally, having heard almost every word of the conversations between my mentor and me, followed suit, changing the bubble gum music that was previously the backdrop to life in the cafe to classical music. Anyone who complained was automatically challenged to an arm wrestle.

Unsurprisingly, I never saw a single person take her up on it.

I considered taking up the challenge myself once, but I put that down to the fact that my whole attitude was changing thanks to my brain sending endorphins rushing through my body. The positive education I was feeding my brain was making me a better person. I could see a path from disaster to master starting to form. It was a path that would eventually see me make enough money for my family and lose my dependency on state handouts. At the same time, my time with my mentor was coming to my end. It was hard to believe that three months had passed. It was somewhat harder to believe that in that relatively short space of time, I had learned knowledge that would last my whole life. But, of course, he wasn't done with me yet. Our last sessions were to furnish me with even more valuable skills - further fresh skills that I could use to magnetise my brain and empower myself to achieve more.

He delved deeper into the need for me to invest in myself using self-discipline. Despite spending the last three months listening to this guy, I, once again, didn't fully understand. And, once again, he was kind enough to explain further. 'John,' he said, 'there are many people in this world who want nice things, but they don't want to pay the price. He meant that they don't want to put in the hard work. They want to do as little as possible yet expect their boss to pay their full wage. They want to do a quick six-month apprenticeship and be paid the same as a 25-year time-served tradesman. They won't pay the price required to succeed, instead choosing to stay in their comfort zone. They watch TV instead of reading books and drink to entertainment themselves yet can't understand why they are so angry with life as a result. If only people were to invest the same amount of time in their brain as they do their car, they would be financially secure. They are happy to spend £200 a month on their car which will one day be little more than a rusting heap of metal on a scrap heap. If they were to invest the same amount of effort in gaining new knowledge and skills, becoming unstoppable is guaranteed. People would be more in control of their lives and have optimistic about their future.

My mentor told me that more than anything else, I had to learn not to do what other people do. I must avoid the urge to invest in material things like gadgets, trendy clothing, and cars, at least for the time being, and concentrate instead of increasing my skills and knowledge. The giant inside me was well and truly starting to stir, a feeling that was somewhat encouraged by the words of Big Sally, who as usual had been listening in, as she shouted, "Now go get 'em, big boy"!

My mentor said I must grab and invest in any opportunity that came my way in the ways of lectures and training. The brain takes in information through the five senses - auditory, visual, kinaesthetic, smell and taste, and when you mix with people with the same mindset, you learn even more. You pick up new ideas and knowledge by actively listening to them and the tutor, by doing mind maps of what you learn and by networking. This is such a great way to learn and one which you should seek out at every opportunity you get. If you take on the challenge, it will change your world. Imagine this - young children use the five senses to learn over 300 different things before the age of five. They can do this because they naturally learn in the right way. You should never doubt yourself because you have 100 billion brain cells, five senses to learn with and seven intelligences with which you can explore the world.

My ears noticeably pricked up when my mentor explained how, in 1969, Georgi Lozanov had taught his students 300 new words in one day using accelerated learning methods. By 1979, students were learning 3,000 words in one day. This equates to fluency in a foreign language in just one day. I was stunned and excited but couldn't help but allow my eyes to fill with tears as I thought back to my school days. If my teachers had used these methods, I would perhaps have been able to achieve more. At the very least, they may have stopped thinking of me as thick.

Lozanov had found that students who wanted to learn faster must ensure that the knowledge initially received by the logical left brain is able to transfer to the creative right brain. At the same time, Howard Gardner from Harvard University was doing research on multiple intelligences and their relationship with learning, concluding that if the intelligences were used correctly, the students would be able to learn faster. By learning through fun and enjoyable activities, these students had an advantage over other students who were using traditional learning methods. Simultaneously, research from the Brain Institute at Stanford was indicating that the brain used only two per cent of its 100 billion cells. He made me understand this concept by asking me to imagine he had given me £100,000 to spend in any way I chose to, but I spent only £2,000 of it in my entire life. That is in effect what most humans do. It's a tragedy that is made even worse by the fact that many teachers of traditional education are not aware of the possibilities of multiple intelligences and, thus, so many clever people fail at school.

The Seven Intelligences:

Linguistic Intelligence
Musical Intelligence
Logic Intelligence
Spatial Intelligence
Kinaesthetic Intelligence
Interpersonal Intelligence
Intrapersonal Intelligence

All this left me in state of shock because, of course, what he was really saying was that I didn't have to leave school at 14½ feeling like a complete thicko. It was just that my brain wasn't synchronised with the teacher's style of teaching. If only my teachers had employed alternative teaching styles, my time at school would have been so much more rewarding, and I would not have gone on to experience such misery.

Tears of Goodbye

It was our last session, and it was time for him to go. He had taught me the three principles of lifelong learning. As he stood to leave, he had that glow of a person who had achieved something he had set out to achieve. He had made such a massive difference in my life already. He was truly a shining star in my dark night of the soul. I felt bereft as tears started to well in my eyes. Here was a man who had gladly given up his time to help without anything but a few bacon butties in return. He was my saviour. I felt somewhat unsure how I would survive without his guidance yet, somehow, I knew that I would in fact thrive. I vowed I would not let him down.

He gave me some last words. "John, if you want a better life, remember the four Ds."

These are:

Desire: Have the burning desire to be the very best that you can be. Understand in your heart that all problems, hurts and setbacks can be overcome. Once you have the desire in your belly, nothing will ever stop you again. Desire will make you unstoppable.

Decide: Make a decision to be happier, more successful and to have a better life. The reason so many people don't is that they fail to decide to do so.

Determination: Don't quit on your dreams and hopes. The stars will shine brighter in the darkest of nights.

Discipline: Have the discipline to do the things you promised to do even if you don't want to do them. Be disciplined with your education, your values and your thoughts and your future life will take care of itself.

"You have been a good pupil, John. I believe in you." And with that, I was watching him walk out of the cafe door and out of my life. I would never see that man again.

Big Sally also took a moment to watch him leave and, upon noticing the tears in my eyes, walked over to me, put her dishcloth down and gave me a big hug. Loosening her grip, she banged on the table and told me not to worry. "You're not so bad; we all feel lost at times, even me. I know I seem overbearing, but I'm as scared as you are about the future. I have three kids to bring up on my own. Now, you tight git, how about a tip?"

A message to my Professor:

I have gone on to use the techniques you taught me to great advantage in my own life and those of others. I have used my car as a university on wheels. I have read for an hour each day while listening to Baroque music. I have disfigured more books than I care to mention. I have transformed from disaster to master, from a shy young fellow who automatically sat in the back row to a confident man who teaches all over the world. You gave that to me. You were the one person to see the fading light in my eyes and resolve to do something about it. You are always in my heart.

A message to Big Sally:

If you are reading this, I hope you have found a man who has given you the love you deserve, and I hope your children appreciate the long hours you put in to give them a good standard of living. To this day, I still believe I would have beaten you at an arm wrestle. And yes, I can hear the words, "In your dreams, big boy ringing in my ears."

Were you Paying Attention?

I really did fly with the eagles with the professor and Sally. Put the knowledge from your short-term memory into your long-term memory

1. Where did I meet my professor?
2. What time did we meet each week and where?
3. Leaders are ….
4. If you read for one hour each day, that equates to how many books each year?
5. How and why do you disfigure a book?
6. Who threatened to throw me out of a window and why?

7. What sort of books should you read?
8. How can you make your car a university on wheels?

3. THE SECRET OF BAD AND GOOD HABITS

'If your actions inspire others to dream more, learn more, do more, and become more, then you are a leader.' John Quincy Adams

Being told that I was nothing but a thick scouser left me feeling that the world was cruel and sad place and that everyone in it was better than me. Redundancy had left me worried sick about how I would pay the mortgage and feed my family.

I would go to the pub, only to see my so-called friends turn their backs on me because they knew I wouldn't have the money to buy a round. It's hardly surprising that all this worry led me to develop low self-esteem, no belief in myself and a huge lack of confidence. Determined, and thinking that otherwise I would head towards either total depression or a nervous breakdown, I was told to look for help. I was told not to get into drugs and become a homeless bum.

I wanted desperately to move away from the dark night of the soul and see a better future for myself. I set out to find someone who would help.

Then like a bright star, Brian came into my life, it was an outside chance, I would now call it serendipity.

I was told that he was always so positive and read books about the habits of the mind.

So, I begged him as a fellow scouser to help me. And that's the great beauty of people from Liverpool; they always respond to a cry for help.

Like the good person he was, Brian encouraged me in the first instance to talk freely about my life and problems. His focused and rather awkward questions led him to the conclusion that I had picked up some seriously bad behavioural habits in my journey through life, thus far. Upon asking him how such habits were formed, Brian explained that our brain is like a sponge, particularly in our formative years. We learn to speak a particular language and develop certain behaviours by copying the language and behaviours of others. We file everything away for future use, regardless of whether it is good or bad.

I was initially confused by this concept and could almost see Brian thinking to himself 'what do these people actually learn in school?'. He pressed on regardless by explaining that each time we engage in an activity, the brain records that activity and places a pathway into the subconscious part of the brain. When you repeat that same activity later, the brain remembers and calls upon the recorded pathway - the path of least resistance. He likened the process to that of a river running down a mountain - the water will always take the path of least resistance on its journey to the bottom of the mountain. The brain is powerful and wants to help us achieve anything we desire. Activities become orders that the brain follows, and it does so by using the same pathway over and over again, resisting all temptation to do anything differently. The pathway that the brain forms and uses are what psychologists refer to as a neural groove. Each time an activity is repeated, the neural groove is reinforced and becomes stronger. Ultimately, the pathway becomes so strong that it becomes a rut. In turn, that rut becomes a comfort zone. Habits, whether good or bad, are formed simply by the brain's determination to use the same neural grooves.

The Beatles

In a more recent conversation with Brian, he asked me who my favourite singers were and, of course, I said The Beatles. Brian told me that the so-called fab four had recorded their song Love Me Do over 50 years ago, asking me whether the voices of John Lennon and Paul McCartney would still sound the same now as it did then. Now it was my turn to think Brian wasn't all that bright, but he soon proved me wrong when he explained that their voices would forever sound the same because of the grooves in which they were laid. "Don't you see, John?" he said, "People who get into a habit of self-doubt, or being miserable, or smoking or heavy drinking, will continue those habits for long periods of time, often until the day they die."

He went on to ask if I had ever been to a school reunion. I had, of course, and knew many others who had also done so. Brian explained that research had shown that when old school friends met up for the first time after 20, 30 and even 40 years, the first thing out of the mouths is often to exclaim that their old mate looks great and that they hadn't changed a bit. Of course, that is a lie - 40 years can lead to some pretty dramatic changes on the outside. When questioned after the event by researchers, those same people spoke the truth. There had, in fact, been noticeable changes in how their old friends looked. It was their personality that had not changed. They still told the same old corny jokes and had the same mannerisms. This is evidence of neural grooves at work. 'You see, John, once a habit is formed, then we will carry on singing the same old song forever.' I listened with amusement as Brian proceeded with a chorus of Love Me Do.

Neural Grooves

Brian was eager to understand how many pathways or neural grooves I had formed, and so he requested that I draw up a list of daily, weekly and monthly habits. If you wish to identify what is slowing your career progress, preventing you from earning money, ruining your health and stopping you from enjoying loving relationships, I strongly suggest you write your own list. When reviewing mine, it immediately became clear why I was overweight, concerned about bills, constantly arguing and suffering from a lack of energy. I was stunned. There were some positives on my list, but the negatives far outweighed those things I had been doing that were helping me to lead a better life. After I wondered out loud about how long it had taken me to form these habits, Brian explained that it took between 21 and 30 days to form a new neural pathway in the brain. Feeling clever, I suggested that with a concerted effort to form new success habits over the next 30 days, I would be able to ditch the ones that were holding me back. Brian felt that my idea had potential but warned that I had been practising my bad habits for years. As such, they would always be lurking in the background, waiting for the opportunity to force my behaviour back on their former pathway - the path of least resistance. This is why smokers still occasionally desire a cigarette even years after quitting.

To form new pathways and develop new good habits requires that a person has the discipline to practice deep repetition for a magical 30-day period. If you can exhibit the strong discipline such an attempt requires, you will have a chance to start living the life you richly deserve. Although Brian was quick to explain that many people before me had tried this approach but lacked the discipline to see it through, the idea that I could start to practice the same behaviours as successful people did, and achieve the same results, was a source of excitement to me. Brian had, however, said something that really scared me. He told me that the brain of people who had thought about the same thing for many years would resist any attempt to change and do its level best to stay in its comfort zone. Yet if I didn't form new and better habits, I was doomed to carry on struggling. I was determined to succeed.

Despite my best intentions, I found it so hard to implement change when left to my own devices. In truth, I found the whole process rather like a game of snakes and ladders. I would take a few steps forward and then a few steps back. My subconscious was resisting my efforts and kept trying to move back into its former comfort zone. Brian had warned me that this would happen, using the example that we all feel excitement and determination when we start something new, but it doesn't take long for our resolve to fade. This is perhaps most obvious when we make New Year's resolutions only to find that by late February, we are back to our old ways. In short, the brain has won.

It has been successful in its attempt to drag us back to our bad habits. My friend who runs a gym once told me something similar, explaining how new members would sign up in their droves each January having overindulged over Christmas. They were so eager to lose weight and get fit and would happily pay a year in advance, but they would never keep it up. They were stranger to the gym by February. Taking that 12-month initial payment, however, was like taking candy from a baby.

In my next session with this wise old man, Brian, I told him about the problems I had been having. His response was to stand up and flap his arms while making a clucking noise. As you imagine, I thought the guy had completely lost it. This was one habit that I felt my mentor should abandon immediately. However, far from completely losing the plot, what Brian was trying to get through to me was that a hen could display the kind of discipline that a human often found so difficult. A hen must sit on its eggs for 21 days before the chicks are able to hatch. Should the hen fail to sit on its eggs for the required period, the chicks will never appear. Numerous studies and experiments have shown, however, that hens are fiercely protective of their eggs. Even in the face of danger, for example, when a fox sneaks into the hen house, the hen will remain on her nest. This anecdote refreshed my determination to change my habits. If a hen could do it, then I was damn sure that I could.

Fear or Gain

To help me out, Brian used the principle of fear and gain to explain that while it wouldn't be easy to change my habits from bad to good, the process would be easier if I imagined what would happen if I failed to change my ways and, conversely, the gains I could make if I were successful. In other words, how my life could change for the better if I managed to change my habits. Brian asked me to write down all the new habits I wanted to form. I couldn't help but feel excited, as I wrote. I knew that if I could form new neural grooves, my life would change dramatically. When I reached my senior years, I would still have the same successful habits. Boy, when I went to that school reunion, they would see a different John Haynes. I went on to develop new successful habits which, to this day, have served me well. These habits are now so deeply ingrained in my subconscious mind that I feel out of my comfort zone if I do not do them. These habits were formed in a relatively short space of time yet remain an important part of life thanks to the neural pathways I formed years ago.

My new habits:

1. Introduce daily exercise into my life by walking for three miles each morning. This helps me to clear my head for the day ahead, not to mention burning calories from my body.
2. Read each morning, always on a subject that would better my life, help me to save time or make money or improve my relationships. Reading to the mind is like exercise to the body.
3. Plan each day in advance using the A-B-C-D-E technique (E is for eliminate). A must be completed first, B is only to be done after A is completed, and C only after B. D is for delegation. Delegate a task back to the person who gave the work to you or delegate to a junior who is paid less than you. If you want to be on £100 hour, don't do £10 an hour work.

Additionally, over the years, I have developed my five core values. These habits have helped me to make great decisions and to live my life in a way that I can be proud of.

1. Honesty and integrity
2. Family
3. Career
4. Health
5. Self-Development

Throughout our sessions, my wise old man pushed me, encouraged me and even shouted at me to force me to form new habits. He helped me to find the discipline I would need to change my bad habits into successful habits and, in doing so, he changed my life forever. Sure, he was a right ball ache at times but looking back he was the one person who I will be eternally grateful to for the rest of my life. He showed me the true value of self-discipline.

Socrates

I recall a story Brian told me about the classical Greek philosopher Socrates to illustrate how poor habits can lead to us wasting so many opportunities in our life. A young disciple had asked Socrates how he could become rich, famous and respected. The young boy wondered why he must wait until he became old in years to achieve such things. Socrates replied that all people want the best things in life, but few are willing to pay the price. He said that we must all put in the long hours, invest in our education and commit to self-discipline to achieve our goals and dreams. We all have the same opportunities, but bad habits cause individuals to throw those opportunities away. How many opportunities have you thrown away?

Sow and Reap

The young disciple persisted by saying that he didn't want to wait so long. He wanted fame, fortune and recognition now. He promised Socrates that, if he gave him the advice he so desperately wanted, he would not throw the opportunity away. Socrates relented and told the young boy that the biggest diamond in the world lay on the shores of Greece. Once the boy found the diamond, he would have the fame and fortune he sought. The boy was ecstatic, but Socrates warned him to curb his enthusiasm. The diamond would not be easy to find for it was encased in the shell of a large stone. The boy cried out in disbelief 'But, Socrates, how will I find it? There are thousands of stones on the shore!'. Socrates informed the young boy that the stone in question was a "touchstone". When the boy picked the right stone up, it would burn his hand. All the boy had to do then was crack the stone open. The diamond would then be his.

Elated, the boy wasted no time in heading to the beach. It was there that he got a sense of just how big his task would prove to be. There were so many stones that he didn't immediately know where to start. He decided to pick up the large stones one by one. If it didn't burn his hand, he would simply throw it into the sea to avoid picking up the same stone later on. All day long, he picked up stones and threw them into the sea. He had no luck that day, but it didn't deter him from trying again. Ultimately the boy spent months on that beach, continually throwing the stones that did not burn his hand into the sea. Eventually, he picked up a stone that was hot to the touch. His mind went on red alert, screaming touchstone, touchstone, touchstone. His subconscious, however, instructed him to throw the stone into the sea. A split second after he had done so he realised what he had done. He had thrown his opportunity away just like that. Like us all, how many opportunities have you thrown away in your personal life and career? It's all down to habit.

The boy sobbed uncontrollably as he walked wearily back to his village, all the while praying he would not see Socrates. The last thing he wanted to hear was 'I told you so!'. Of course, Murphy's Law (what will go wrong will happen at the worst possible time) meant that Socrates was the first person he saw on his arrival at his village. 'Come here, young man. Tell me, did you grab the opportunity I gave you to achieve fame and fortune?'. The young boy burst out crying again, tearfully explaining what had happened on the beach. Socrates listened patiently before saying to this poor demented soul that he had succumbed to the power of habits. The boy had, however, learned a great lesson - he had thrown the stones into the sea so many times it had formed a habit. There are no shortcuts in life. He must pay the price for everything in hard work.

The story about Socrates and the young man made me think

about how my bad habits had held me back in life. I thought of all the time I had wasted in front of the TV instead of educating myself by reading a book. I thought of the time I had spent with negative people and how that had led me to become a negative person myself. I had stayed in jobs I hated working for bosses I didn't respect. In doing so, I had returned home to my family in a bad mood every night, taking my frustrations out on them and making their lives unhappy. I had thrown many touchstones back in the ocean. How about you?

My Shame of a New Habit

To further your understanding of the power of neural pathways, I will share with you a personal experience from years later, one that turned out to be one of the most embarrassing moments of my life. At the time, I was spending full days each Friday and Saturday delivering my master coach programme to career people and entrepreneurs. In an effort to avoid a post-lunch slump on training days, I always eat light - consisting mainly of fruit and water for both breakfast and lunch. While this helps me to stay focused and sharp throughout the day, it does, of course, mean that by the end of the day, I typically feel famished. Because of this, I had developed a habit of going to a local restaurant, The Bar & Grill, each Friday evening for a drink, arriving around 6.30 pm and leaving at 8.30 pm. One particular Friday, after leaving The Bar & Grill, despite eating while I was there, I still felt hungry. A mild hunger pang quickly turned into a feeling that I would starve to death if I didn't get more food immediately. I resolved to rush home as quickly as I could and, in my haste, I took a shortcut. That's when I saw it, gleaming like an oasis in a desert, a branch of Subway.

Well, as you can imagine, I couldn't get in there quick enough, bounding up to the counter like I hadn't eaten in years and looking rather like a kid keen to spend every last bit of their pocket money in a sweet shop. I order the biggest sub I could see on the menu, with all the trimmings, topping up my order with a few packets of crisps and a large coke. As I sat down, to eat, it was all I could do to stop joyous tears from spilling out. I had been saved from starvation by a sandwich!

The very next week as I left The Bar and Grill, the thought of visiting Subway popped into my head and, following the path of least resistance in my mind, I immediately resolved to stop by for a quick sub on the way home, and went on to enjoy another joyous meal. This carried on for five weeks, becoming a routine as regular as dunking a biscuit in my cup of tea. I was well aware that I was succumbing to a bad habit and was rather annoyed with myself for doing so. After all, I taught others about the dangers of bad habits and how easy it was to fall under their spell. However, I decided to use my personal experience as additional material for the course I was delivering. I didn't know it at the time, but the decision to share my experience with the course attendees would prove to be a foolish one, as it turned out, especially so because of the presence of the Mounty brothers - two lads from Liverpool that you just didn't mess with. To give you an indication of what's to come, I must tell you that on all my courses, I tell participants about the importance of being willing to make a positive difference in other people's lives, teaching them that a mind in motion will stay in motion unless an outside force destroys it.

I Told Lies

When Friday evening rolled around once again, I indulged in my habit of heading to The Bar & Grill after finishing at the office. As I walked through the doors, I was somewhat surprised to see every delegate on the current course standing at the bar. My heart told me I was glad to see them, but, as the song goes, my mind told me that there was trouble ahead. As usual, I spent a couple of hours in The Bar & Grill, this time laughing and joking with the course delegates as opposed to my usual buddies. Around 8.30 pm, I announced I was heading off. In harmony - and as if they had been waiting for this moment all day - the whole team in unison asked me where I was going. Somewhat surprised by their enthusiastic question, I nervously responded that I was going home. 'And where else are you going?' they boomed. It suddenly dawned on me that the team had, in fact, been waiting for this moment all day. Led by the Mounty brothers, they had taken it upon themselves to interrupt my mind in motion and put a stop to my newfound urge for a Friday night sub. Of course, at this point, I was still determined to head to Subway. All I had to do was figure out how to get past these delegates, who were by now starting to resemble a pack of wolves moving in for the kill. I said once again I was going home, but the neural groove in my mind said, 'No, you're not, you're going to Subway.' Bloody habits!

But the strong Mounty brothers and the team had other ideas; they lifted me up off my feet and took me to the door and shouted for a taxi. I was furious! Everybody in the bar was laughing, but the Mounty brothers were totally focused on getting me home and stopping my bad habit of going to Subway. They warned the taxi driver; he was to take me straight home because in Liverpool you don't muck about with the Mounty brothers.

The taxi took off, and I looked back; I could see the gang all watching the taxi. Once out of sight of them, I screamed at the driver to take me to Subway. Do you see? I was totally out of my comfort zone of not sticking to my habit.

The taxi driver said, 'I am not going to cross the Mounty brothers.' So, I had to bribe him, and gave him double the fare. So, there I was telling lies, paying extra just to stay in my comfort zone. When I got to Subway, I wasn't even hungry, but the waitress saw me coming in, and out of habit (again), had my huge subway order waiting for me. I sat in my usual seat and started to eat, thinking about those naughty Mounty brothers, and the team, embarrassing me in front of everyone in The Bar & Grill.

I Died Inside

And then it happened. My biggest nightmare came about. The Mounty brothers and the rest of the team marched into Subway.

They were sharper than me and knew my habit would sneakily take me to Subway.

They had caught me red-handed. They screamed at me, "You lied to us John Haynes, you said you were going home."

The Mounty brothers picked up my tray and said to the waitress, 'You eat this love, this lying get is going home.' I was so red and embarrassed, I said, 'Boys, I am so sorry,' but they were having none of it, they got me into another taxi, and screamed, 'Home James.'

I looked back again at them; they were all laughing and giving each other high-fives; they were so pleased with themselves.

The next day in class they had drawn a big sign on the board which said:

'A mind in motion will stay in motion until it's disturbed by an outside force.' They had signed it, The Mounty Brothers and The Team.

They joked and laughed all day about the incident. I was so ashamed but laughed along with them and thanked them all so much for breaking my habit.

Even now when I pass Subway, I can see images of the Mounty brothers standing there saying, "On your way John Haynes."

So, you see habits are easily formed good or bad. I am now still great friends with the Mounty brothers. I thank them so much; for reminding me that habits, good or bad, are just pathways in the brain. They could be there for the rest of your life if you don't have friends to help get rid of them.

As for Brian, he totally saved me and successfully changed my life. You are an inspirational man Brian, thank you so much.

Questions for You

1. What are the two emotions we make decisions on? Fear and _____
2. How many days does it take to form a habit?
3. What are JHJ core values?
4. What proves hens have strong discipline habits?
5. How are habits proved at school reunions?

6. Why do people keep bad habits?
7. What is a comfort zone?
8. Write ten bad habits that you have formed.
9. Write ten success habits you have formed.
10. What were the names of the people that helped me break my bad habits?

'The starting point of all achievement is desire. Weak desires bring weak results, just as a small fire makes a small amount of heat.' Napoleon Hill.

4. HOW TO DEAL WITH OBNOXIOUS, BULLYING AND DIFFICULT PEOPLE

If you do not do the thing you fear, the fear controls your life. Leap and the net will appear.

'Sometimes you just have to take the leap and build your wings on the way down.' Kobi Yamada.

From the day I left school, I did not realise that to have a happy life you have to learn to deal with negative, difficult people. So, let me share with you with some of the things I have learnt along the long road of my life. I also passed this knowledge on when I was a director of a large company, and then went on to become an executive coach and mentor. All the knowledge I learnt from the professor certainly paid off.

A survey of wonderful, older people aged 85 and over asked them to reflect upon their lives and recall the successes and failures of their experience. The answers revealed a factor that was common to all recipients – the pain and misery caused by obnoxious bullies. Those surveyed expressed regret that they had not stood up to the bullies but had instead allowed them to get away with causing the unhappiness and stress that went with this negative behaviour. I think that it is apparent that 85 per cent of our problems talk back to us.

I want you to understand the effect that negative behaviour patterns have on others and how it is possible to counteract it when you encounter it yourself. I can best explain it by using an example from many years ago when a senior member at the company I worked for at the time asked me to coach a member of his staff - Angela. Angela was underperforming in a junior management role and seemed to be stressed for much of the time.

Talking Behind Her Back

Although Angela was hesitant to be candid during our initial sessions, and almost seemed to be in denial about the challenges she was clearly experiencing at work; patience, empathy and tact on my part eventually allowed her to develop enough confidence in me to open up and explain what was going on. It turned out that Angela felt she was not suited to management. This feeling was compounded by the fact that the members of staff in her team were always laughing at her and talking about her behind her back. They were rude and insulting but clever enough not to cross the line and risk discipline or dismissal. Staff meetings were especially painful; whenever she spoke, her team members would shoot her disparaging looks, would talk over her and challenge her on every point. All this left her feeling like she was constantly under attack and often meant that she left work early just to escape the constant barrage of abuse. Every time she did, she felt like she was telling the bullies that they had won yet again.

Ruined Family Life

Tears rolled down her face as she explained that she couldn't sleep at night and that her weekends were taken over by depressing thoughts about the insults and rudeness that would inevitably take place over the following week. She was concerned about the effect it was having on her family. Her husband and children couldn't help but notice her increasingly long face and vacant expression. It was obvious that the current state of affairs meant that Angela was simply incapable of giving her family the love and attention they deserved. She was being dragged down by it all and felt unable to confront these obnoxious, bullying employees.

The bullying toward Angela had become so severe she had reached her wits end, and also believed that she was not the right person for the job. She had understandably become to dread showing up to work but continued to work in this toxic environment regardless. She did so because she was committed to supporting her family whose finances would not cope with the loss of income that would result from Angela quitting her job. We all go the extra mile for the people we love. It's the reason we get up and go to work every day even if we don't like our colleagues. Our love for our family almost always overrides any other concerns we might have, and Angela was no different.

Pack of Wolves

My interpretation of this situation was that this group of employees were behaving like a pack of wolves descending upon their prey. As a result, Angela's self-esteem was on the floor. She had developed significant doubts in her abilities and her daily life, even when she wasn't at work, was pervaded by constant negative thoughts. This was a truly sad case of emotional bullying that needed immediate action on my part. If my response was delayed in any way, Angela's situation would continue to worsen. In the first instance, I would need to speak to members of senior management at the company who I felt, at best, must be unaware of the problems Angela was facing or, at worst, choosing to ignore her plight. Their reaction was, of course, to claim they did not know at all about the situation but also admitted that they had not offered Angela any training in the three years since she had been promoted to her management role. They came up with the somewhat pathetic excuse that they hadn't been able to afford to provide the appropriate training. It also became evident that Angela had been promoted to management simply because she had been at the company the longest and not because she was particularly suited to the role she was asked to do. The consequence of these oversights was to turn a hardworking and loyal employee into a nervous and worried person who went home every night feeling that her life was worthless.

Many major companies use the S.W.A.N system for selection processes. This had not been the case here. In fact, what had happened here was a gross violation of the selection process. The company had given Angela a role for which she was clearly not suited and subsequently given her no support, training or guidance. Until now, Angela had no-one to turn to for support. She was simply forced to rely on her own reserves which, understandably, had become severely depleted. The management at this company was aware that the section was underperforming. By ignoring the problem, they had not only ignored it but had also aided and abetted Angela's declining state of mind. Their attitude had contributed to an environment where ill health was spiralling, and costs were increasing substantially due to lost working time and a reduction in productivity. This is not a solitary situation and is why all the reports about senior management in this country are saying that it is the worst and most ignorant it has ever been.

Stress is a Killer

Buoyed by my advice that she must begin to stand up for herself, Angela took the brave step of speaking to her doctor about how her problems were causing her to lose out on sleep. She had only wanted a prescription for sleeping pills, but after seeing the stress etched on her face, her doctor wasted no time in issuing Angela with a sick note excusing her from work indefinitely.

They say that stress is one of the biggest killers in the world today. Despite medical science becoming advanced enough to eradicate diseases such as smallpox and typhoid fever, stress has proved to be as resilient as the common cold.

Advice About Courage

Angela remained off work for a full six months before eventually plucking up the courage to seek advice from a solicitor regarding the emotional cruelty she had experienced at work. When I met her again some years later, she told me that she still found it hard to sleep at night due to flashbacks of her awful experience. At that time, I was in a position to offer Angela help to regain her self-confidence. I am also pleased to say that the company learned their lesson. Improved selection processes using the S.W.A.N system were put in place as were new training programmes for all future managers. The preying wolves were given final notices and slowly but surely productivity and staff morale began to improve. It was a much happier place to work. This result shows that if there are negative people in a business, their inclination to moan, gossip and backstab will cause good workers to feel depressed and start to underperform. Thus, one of the secrets of good business is to weed out the negative people and let the positive people fly with the eagles.

Unless they are extremely lucky, everyone will meet a bully in their lifetime. This unpleasant behaviour is not exclusive to the workplace. You can encounter a bully at home, among your neighbours and friendship groups and even at school. The effects of a bully in your life can be significant. Just think about how Angela's life was so adversely affected and how she continued to suffer years after the abuse had taken place. So how can you overcome this kind of behaviour? How should you treat a bully? Let's explore some tactics.

Learning to Confront a Bully

There is a direct relation between the amount of control you have in your life and how positive you feel. The more control you have, the happier you will be. In Angela's case, she had lost all control over her own life and had become ruled by negative emotions. In every situation like this, the antidote is to accept responsibility. Look at the reasons why you may be responsible for what has happened. In Angela's case, her responsibility lay in her failure to seek training in how to deal with difficult people.

Peace of mind is one of the most important things to have in life. To have it, you must learn how to get along with people from diverse backgrounds in a variety of situations. And yes, this includes people who are downright rude and obnoxious. It is the hallmark for future happiness at work and at home. This is borne out by great leaders and psychologists and from people who have experienced it for themselves. It brings the famous saying from Shakespeare's 16th-century play Hamlet to mind. *'Take arms against a sea of troubles. And, by opposing, end them.'* This advice is as relevant today as it was five centuries ago.

Negative Emotions

I, myself, have experienced feelings of hopelessness and a lack of control in my life. I could identify with Angela as I too, had once held everything inside. However, we must learn to stand up for ourselves and unburden our problems for if we do not, the only option is to carry them around with us. So, take arms and confront your problems. It is the only way. We all have an immune system, but what you may not realise is that our immune systems feed on our emotional state, be it positive or negative. The negative emotional state weakens the body and affects our health. We begin to experience a general feeling of debility and become susceptible to ailments such as coughs, colds and headaches. Psychologists state that 'whatever the mind harbours, the body expresses!' This is what is referred to as a psychosomatic illness. If, on the other hand, we fill our minds with positive thoughts, mix with positive people, say positive affirmations, visualise positive things and have clear written goals, then the immune system becomes stronger. It is our choice.

Low Self-Esteem

In my opinion, our ability to act in this way starts in early childhood when we are often subjected to conditional love by our parents, even if is it done so unknowingly. Love withheld in our early years creates a pathway for low self-esteem, which, in turn, lowers self-belief and increases our reluctance to confront situations. Negativity is experienced in early childhood in the form of the seemingly constant use of the words, No, You're Naughty, or Stop it! As kids we act like kamikaze pilots, exploring the world, touching objects, screaming and shouting and generally getting into what our long-suffering parents deemed mischief. Their reprimands came from the right place in their hearts but would not serve us well in later life. Each time our parents criticised us or got angry with us for jumping around as we had just won the lottery, we experienced deep feelings of guilt and unworthiness. The message we got from our parents was that if we were naughty, they could withdraw their love. As a result, we stop exploring the world, we stop asking questions, and we lose our brave spirit. We feel inferior and inadequate and, unfortunately, we carry these feelings with us into later life and inevitably develop an inability to confront any bullies that may come into our lives and seek to control us.

From personal experience, I know how easy it is to find yourself in a work or home environment where you are unhappy but reluctant to confront the situation. You make all sorts of excuses – I am scared, I might get the sack, my boss might get angry, the neighbours won't talk to me – just to avoid taking responsibility. Yes, in my short life, I have indeed encountered many situations like the one Angela found herself in. In fact, when I was coaching Angela, I was often reliving the pain of my own previous troubles. I just did not like to confront. I wouldn't take arms against the sea of troubles.

Cut My Stomach Open

Years later, it all caught up with me. I had the flu and was taking aspirin for it when my health took a sudden turn for the worse. I was rushed to the hospital only to find out that what I thought was the flu was a perforated ulcer which had been bleeding for days. I immediately underwent an operation, during which I nearly died three times. This was the 80s, after all. There was no laser surgery back then. The surgeon had cut my stomach wide open, and I still have a 12-inch scar to prove it. The surgeon told me afterwards that it was because of my stressful lifestyle; which included not confronting people. Thankfully, it had nothing to do with my drinking.

If I wanted to live, I would have to change my life. But what had caused me to dislike confrontation? The answer was simple. It was stress. I had let people walk all over me. I had not only failed to stand up for myself, but rather, I had begun to let the negative people, and the bullies and their criticism of me, weaken me. In doing so, I had weakened my immune system. Blimey, I thought, I must stop letting the sun go down on arguments and stop leaving problems to fester in my mind for if I don't, I will be back at this hospital in big trouble.

I learned later – and this is what I ultimately shared with Angela – that there are three types of significant behaviour and over our lifetimes, it is possible for us to exhibit the signs of all three.

1. Passive
2. Aggressive
3. Assertive

Passive Behaviour

People who exhibit passive behaviour are usually very easy to get along with and for good reasons. They are the first to lend a hand or do a favour. They aim to please and will likely never confront a situation. They keep their frustrations to themselves and would sooner be liked and respected. They are often the people who were brought up thinking that the love from their parents was conditional. Angela agreed that she was most likely to indulge in passive behaviour.

Aggressive Behaviour

Aggressive people are the exact opposite of those with passive behaviour traits. They are usually quite awkward people and often lean toward being rude, difficult, moody and bullying towards others. If they fail to get their own way, they tend to resort to guilt techniques such as sulking and the silent treatment to get what they want. Angela and I both agreed that this didn't describe her but did describe the people in her team.

Have you noticed a common factor between passive and aggressive behaviours? They both have low self-esteem, low self-worth and low self-confidence. Aggressive people need to domineer passive people to feel better about themselves.

Assertive Behaviour

In comparison, assertive people are neither passive nor aggressive. They are their own people. They can stand up for themselves without shouting or bullying. They are calm and able to make any point in a reasonable manner. To be assertive is a master skill and one which takes many hours to achieve. As with other skills, though, such as learning to drive or to speak a new language, you can pick up a skill simply by practising at every opportunity. This dedicated practice will bring forward a positive outcome. Assertive people aim for mental strength, and they often do this by starting each day with a golden hour. They practice affirmations daily and are committed to their ongoing education.

Principles of Assertiveness

Learning to be assertive will lead to a happier life at home, work and play. You will become a good leader and an example to others. If you are looking for a role model, and you want to work on your assertiveness, you need to look at people like Nelson Mandela, Mother Theresa and Muhammad Ali.

There are six principles involved in assertive behaviour:

1. Always use "I" not "You."
2. See it through other's eyes. Feel, felt, found
3. Mental movie approach
4. Broken record
5. Use silence
6. Delay the answer

The "I" Word

At all stages of an encounter with an aggressive person, they are trying to bait you into reacting to their demands. A bully likes nothing better than to ensnare the person they are communicating with to become angry and to react accordingly. This is often what a bully deems a good result. Forcing a person to stoop to their level will massage their ego. Let's take the first principle of always saying I - and not You. An assertive person must avoid saying things like "You are a bad person," or, "You are rude," as these will be taken as a personal insult. By replacing You with I, by saying things like, "I am not happy with your behaviour," you can immediately disarm almost any situation. By taking responsibility, you are not attacking the bully personally, you leave them struggling as to what to say in response. You have taken the control of the situation away from the bully and placed it firmly in your own hands. Use the starters - I am, I think, or I feel - and see how quickly you can turn a bad situation into a much better one.

I am reminded of an example from my own life. I was holding a full-day seminar one Saturday, and as I was going through accelerated learning techniques, I somehow managed to break the strap on one of my valuable watches. I decided to go to a jewellery store during the lunch break. I was running late as I entered the shop and, despite a lovely shop assistant by the name of Cheryl assuring me that the broken strap would take no more than a few minutes to fix, I felt unable to wait. I told Cheryl I would return in a few days to collect the watch and I dashed back to my waiting class. Well, as I'm sure you're aware, life can get in the way of the best-laid plans and a full month had passed before I remembered that I needed to collect my watch.

Indecisiveness

When I returned to the shop, there was a long queue, seemingly caused by the inability of an older woman at the front to choose between a leather or stretch strap for her husband's new watch. The manager, that was serving her, was clearly becoming irritated by her indecisiveness, and the growing queue, and had begun to speak to her in an increasingly irate manner. In the end, he all but shouted at the poor woman that he was trying to run a business and that she should hurry up and decide on a strap because a queue had built up behind her. The poor woman clearly had been unaware that other customers were waiting and rushed out of the shop; apologising to everyone as she went. This was a clear example of an aggressive person going up against a passive person, so it will probably be of little surprise to hear that I didn't like what I had witnessed.

Upon reaching the front of the queue, I handed my receipt to this unpleasant man who, after glancing at it, shouted into the back to Cheryl for "Mr Haynes' watch." A nervous Cheryl replied that it wasn't ready. With one eye already on the next customer, he repeated what Cheryl had said. His dismissive attitude and lack of a proper explanation made the hairs on the back of my neck stand on end. "But it's been a month," I said. "And I was told it was a simple one-minute job. Why isn't it ready?" Mr Hargreaves then used the same loud and aggressive tone he had used on the older woman to tell me to move aside so that he could serve the next customer.

I'm not sure what came over me, but I responded to him as quickly as a boxer giving his opponent a series of swift jabs in the ring. "I believe your manners are appalling. I feel you are a very rude person. The way you treated that old lady disgusted me, and I feel that you should be ashamed of yourself. I predict your business will be in trouble if you carry on this way." Bloody hell, I thought to myself. Where did that all come from? That I didn't know, but what I did know was that by using the word I and not You, I didn't attract his low self-esteem and low self-worth. In fact, the only response he could come up with was to shout to Cheryl to, "Come and sort this out." And with that, he retreated to sulk behind his computer at the other side of the store.

Apprehensive

Another week passed before I had a chance to return to the shop but have to confess that I was more than a little apprehensive about the reception that was in store for me. I was half-expecting World War 3 to break out because of what I had said the previous week. Face to face with my new nemesis once again, he gave my pathetic little wave a stern look and, once again, shouted to Cheryl to, "Come and serve Mr Haynes." The delightful Cheryl came running from the back room, watch in hand, with an apology for the repair having taken so long. The fix had been far more complicated than she had initially thought. I immediately thought that this meant I was about to fork out for a big bill but to my surprise upon asking how much the repairs would cost, Cheryl told me, with a somewhat triumphant look on her face, "Well, that's the best bit, Mr Haynes. Mr Hargreaves has waived the cost of the repairs due to the delay." I instantly shouted across the room "Well, that's very kind of you, Mr Hargreaves." He responded with a friendly nod as Cheryl proudly returned the watch to my wrist, clearly over the moon that it was all sorted.

To this day, I believe that had I used the word You instead of I when reprimanding Mr Hargreaves, the outcome would have been very different. As it was, the situation turned out for the best because someone had stood up to him in an assertive way. Perhaps he may have even thought twice about using his bad manners and bullying tactics when he next met an indecisive old lady. Never back away from bullies. Just use the "I" word.

See It Through Others' Eyes

This is a great way to act assertively. When somebody is rude and trying to upset you, don't go down to their level, after all, wrong assumptions are the cause of every misunderstanding. Just try to understand why they were acting this way. It could be they have just lost a big client, or money, or their job and they are trying to take it out on you.

Rise above it and use the boomerang effect. Just say, "I know exactly how you feel, if I was in your situation I would be acting and feeling the same." Say these immortal words three times, and you see the aggressive person change straight away. They think, "Yes you would be thinking and acting just like me." The boomerang effect works. They calm down and start thinking at least somebody, at last, understands me. Now that's being assertive.

Use the Mental Movie Approach

Before an uncomfortable situation, a stressful meeting or an argument ready to explode, just close your eyes and go into Alpha Theta state; walk it through in your mind. Visualise the perfect outcome. The pictures you see will be the person you will be. Visualise being assertive. Your mind is like a giant magnet; it will draw everything into your life, that you see and visualise. Like a magnet pulls in a pile of iron filings.

The Broken Record

The brain has got to hear words three or four times before it takes things seriously. It all stems back from early childhood. Remember when we used to ask our parents for ice cream, and they flatly said no, but we persisted; repeating it four or five times until they said yes. The brain always ignores the first one or two words, so, when you are facing a difficult person or a staff member just use the broken record approach, and then you will eventually get through to them.

I remember when I was a senior manager in a big company. One of my members of staff came up to me and asked to go home early as there was a crisis, but because he was always using this excuse to go home early, I said to him, "Geoff, has your grandmother died again for the tenth time?"

He said, "You don't understand boss I need to go home."

So, I used the broken record technique. I said, "Geoff if you clear all your priority work you can go home early."

He became very irate, so I used the broken record technique and repeated myself; "You can go home early after you have completed your priority work."

I had to repeat myself four times. Then Geoff, after hearing me four times suddenly said, "Boss, if I finish my priority work then can I go home early?"

That's how habits in the brain work, so don't get angry when people don't do as you ask the first time. Just repeat yourself and use the broken record technique.

The Silence

This is what bullies hate the most. When a person is pushing for an argument or trying to make you say something you might regret have the courage to use silence; say, "I understand how you feel, but I have nothing more to say on this subject." Then go completely quiet.

It doesn't matter how much they shout or scream. Just stay silent. They hate it but admire you later for having the will-power to stay silent. Have the willpower and courage not to be dragged down to their level. Simply say, "I understand exactly how you feel, but I have nothing more to say on this matter."
If they persist, repeat the same message: put your finger to your lips and be quiet. Just persist in the silence, and you will feel like a winner, and the rude, nasty person will go away feeling defeated.

Delay, Delay

The Japanese call this the cruellest form of denial. Have you ever made a rash decision and regretted it later on? That's what bullying people try to do; push you or humiliate you into making a decision you're not sure of. Many people have made decisions under pressure and regret it afterwards - a finance deal, a job, buying something from a dishonest salesperson; even getting married. All made bad decisions instead of delaying their decision.

On one of my master coaching seminars, a lady in her fifties shouted, "Bloody hell, John, if I'd only known how to use delaying tactics years ago."

We all asked her to explain; "Well," she said, "I know you won't believe this, boys, but I used to be a pretty 21-year-old girl; 32 years ago. I was excited about life and planning to see the world. I was going out with a boy called Peter, who lived around the corner. It was only puppy love, and I was enjoying life."

She continued, "One day Peter told me that, we were going to a surprise party the following Saturday. I loved parties and asked who the party was for; he told me that it was a surprise and that both sets of our parents were going, and all of our friends. I was very excited."

Her Horrible Surprise

She explained that when they arrived at the restaurant everybody waved at them and seemed so pleased to see them. Remember, at this point, she hadn't known Peter that long and was just having fun. When she asked who the surprise was for, he told her to wait and see. After the meal was over the head waiter placed a magnum of champagne on their table, she thought it was strange, and that all of their friends were giving knowing smiles. The room went quiet as Peter got down on one knee, pulled out an engagement ring, looked her straight in the eye, and proposed.

She was shocked; after all, she felt that she hardly knew him, not enough to marry him. Before she could explain that it was only puppy love and they barely knew each other the restaurant went wild with celebrations. Everybody was standing and clapping and shouting and telling her to say yes. It had all been planned, and she did not have a clue.

She explained how sick it made her feel, the thought of marrying a man that she hardly knew, let alone loved. Then suddenly, his mum jumped up, gave her a big hug, and welcomed her to the family as her new daughter. Then her own mum (not to be outdone), shouted that she would not find a better man. Suddenly, all her friends were and hugging her and saying in unison. "Marry him, marry him."

Marry Me

In a state of shock, a small voice from inside was screaming, "run for it."

But they all wore her down. She felt I didn't want to let everybody down so with the screams ringing in her ears would you believe that she said YES.

The place went wild, they danced and drank champagne all night. Everyone was so pleased.

My class of my students were all opened mouthed; they couldn't believe what they were hearing.

The next morning, she woke up with a hangover, and thought, "Shit, what have I done?" She felt too young to get married, but before she could set things straight, her Mum was around, helping to plan the wedding. She already had a guest list prepared and had chosen a church for the wedding. She was still in a state of shock. Her friends all started to make suggestions for the honeymoon. She got swept away with all the plans, and before she knew it, was married.

She had married a man she didn't know or love and wanted to know where I was with my delay strategies when she needed me. The whole class laughed out loud but showed a lot of sympathy to her.

She explained that after two years, she had her first child, but even before then had gone to her mum and dad to tell them that she was not happy and had made a big mistake. Her mum told her that she had made a lifelong commitment and forbade her to leave the marriage.

So, she put up with it and later had another child. She was never happy, and Peter turned into a drinker and was always moaning.

Wasted Years

Nearly thirty years later, at the age of 51, Anne was combing her hair in the mirror and saw an oldish lady with greying hair. Her mind went back to when she was a young, pretty girl with the world at her feet. She had been full of fun and full of life and had turned into a sad old lady because she made the wrong decision. She hadn't had the courage or the knowledge to delay the decision.

I must of admit there was a lot of sadness in the classroom for

Anne, and a few tears were shed.

That day, when Peter came home, she asked for a divorce. They were not happy together. He didn't give a damn, he put his head down and went back to the pub.

Anne went around to her mother's; unfortunately, her dad had already died. She explained that she had asked for a divorce. Her mum replied that she didn't know why she had married him; and that he wasn't the right man. Even her friends used to say that Peter wasn't the right man.

"So," Anne said, "You see team, I wish I had known that I could delay that decision, then I wouldn't have spent 30 years of my life unhappy."

Everyone in the classroom stood and gave Anne a standing ovation, for sharing her story, and because of her courage and honesty.

But the good news is months later Anne found her real soulmate and is planning to get married again. We were all invited to the wedding.

So, please, please, if you're not sure about any decision. Just delay, delay, delay.

Be assertive and use these words; I would like you to give me twenty-four hours to think it over, or I am sorry I understand how exactly how you feel, but I must have twenty-four hours to think it over.

I promise you after twenty-four hours, with no emotion attached, the decision you make will be the correct one. Now that's being assertive.

So now you know how to deal with rude people, go out and lead a great positive life. People will admire you for your assertive actions.

Eighty-five per cent of problems in life talk back to us. That is "People." But if you know how to deal with these difficult people, then eighty-five per cent of our happiness will talk back to us.

'Fly with eagles and beat all the bullies.'

Test your right-brain memory:

1. How long was Angela off work because of bullying staff?
2. What do nasty people have in common with passive people?
3. What are the three behaviour patterns?
4. Instead of using the You word, what would you replace it with?
5. The wrong assumptions are the root of what?
6. What was the name of the bullying manager who scared the old lady?
7. Children with low self-esteem get brought up with —————— love?
8. What was the name of the selection tool?
9. How many hours do you need to delay a decision?
10. What does the term 'broken record' mean?

The Law of Probabilities

The more different things you try, the more likely it will be you will try the right thing at the right time.

5. HAVE YOU EVER FOUND YOUR SOULMATE?

'The best portion of a good man's life: his little, nameless, unremembered acts of kindness and of love.' William Wordsworth.

As my life proceeded from the dark night of the soul years, I wanted to help people not make the same mistakes that I had made. I decided to be a coach and mentor. After all, I was more experienced; I'd had failures and sad times, but I was on a roll in education.

Many years ago, I coached a young lady by the name of Anna Marie. She was a bubbly and tenacious client who ran a PR company but, as our fortnightly sessions progressed, her personality seemed to change, and she seemed to become steadily less focused on her business.

As with all things in life, our attention is drawn to the things we value the most. In Anna Marie's case, she placed a high value on her love for her fiancée. However, through the course of our sessions, it became clear that there were difficulties in the relationship. As her coach, I wanted to help her resolve her issues and asked whether there was anything I could do to help. Realising my concern for her was genuine, she explained through tears that the love of her life was starting to make her feel unhappy. The poor girl had no idea what she could do to turn the situation around.

Negative Behaviour
Anna Marie explained that her fiancée's behaviour had become very negative and was affecting both her home and business life. Ricky had started to feel jealous of Anna Marie's success and had started acting moody and suspicious, especially if

she returned home late after meetings had run on longer than expected. Anna Marie could no longer enjoy a night out with friends and had to constantly fend off questions about the men with whom she worked. Facing angry questioning about where she had been and who she had been with was starting to become a regular feature in her life.

One incident had caused Anna Marie a great amount of distress. She had won a big PR contract with a major hotel and had arranged a meeting with the hotel's managers. Having sat down to discuss the upcoming work, she happened to glance up, only to see Ricky hiding behind one of the pillars in the hotel lobby. Her fiancée continued to spy on her for the next three hours. Anna Marie felt unable to confide her concerns with any of her colleagues at the meeting and was, instead, left feeling unhappy and distracted throughout the duration of the meeting.

Infidelity

Upon her return home later that day, Anna Marie had confronted Ricky, only to be met with accusations of infidelity and flirting with other men. Despite seemingly managing to convince her fiancée that he was grossly mistaken, the stress of the situation had taken its toll on Anna Marie. In fact, she became so depressed that she took up smoking again, even though she had managed to quit successfully over a year earlier. From that point, Ricky's behaviour had taken a further turn for the worse. He became even more possessive and seemed to want to control Anna Marie's every move. To please him, she had stopped seeing her friends and had even consented to Ricky's request to collect her from work each evening.

Anna Marie explained to me how the situation was making her feel increasingly wretched and constantly on edge. She could no longer talk to Ricky about her work for fear of being spied on again in case she should happen to mention the name of a male colleague. Perhaps even worse, her family and friends had all but stopped visiting her at home because they had tired of Ricky's reaction to seeing Anna Marie enjoying the company of others. It was clear that my client loved her fiancée, but that love was slowly being eroded by fear. She had paid for her love with unhappiness and a deteriorating state of mind. More tears fell from Anna Marie's eyes as she wondered aloud why her previously loving fiancée had suddenly become so jealous of her every move, emphasising her point by saying that she would never even look at another man in the way he suspected.

High Divorce Rate

It is a sad fact that the divorce rate around the world is at a very high level. Even long-term friendships and partnerships are failing because of low self-esteem and low confidence levels. Top psychologists claim that behaviour such as that exhibited by Ricky gives rise to many problems in society, not least crime and alcohol and drug abuse.

Anna Marie's admission had sounded alarm bells ringing for me, and I feared that if this situation was not nipped in the bud, it could quickly turn to violence. Had it become too desperate though? It was clear that to end the relationship would break both their hearts, even if it was probably the best outcome for Anna Marie. I did wonder, though, whether Ricky would turn out to be the kind of guy who would stalk, harass, and threaten Anna Marie should she call time on the relationship. I had every reason to suspect that would be the case. It was clear to me from Ricky's behaviour that he was suffering from low self-esteem, and I asked Anna Marie whether she also felt that might be the case. I explained to her that triggers for gross negativity included jealousy, blame, and feelings of failure and rejection. She looked at me in astonishment as she exclaimed that Ricky was displaying all those behaviours but was still adamant that he was still her great love despite the negativity he was bringing into her life.

Right and Left Brain

In coaching and leadership terms, it is necessary to use the left brain to identify a factual problem and cause before a solution can be reached. To find possible solutions, you must use the creative side of your brain. From there, you choose the best solution, then take the necessary action to put that solution in place.

Left side of the brain – Problem - Cause

Right side of the brain – Solution - Action

If you don't go through this process of using the left brain to identify the problem and cause and the right brain to determine the best solution and the action needed to implement that solution, you will simply end up more confused and may continue to encounter the same specific problem for many years to come. Just look at some of the world's politicians. Many are still facing the same problems as they did many years ago because they never identified the cause.

Early Childhood

I have read that top psychologists recognise the kind of behaviour exhibited by Ricky as having its root cause in early childhood. Such people have been raised in an environment of conditional rather than unconditional love. Parents should never use destructive criticism as a method of interaction with their children. Young people are exceptionally vulnerable to criticism of any kind. It tears them up inside. Destructive criticism has, probably, had a worse effect of personalities than any other thing in history. Most of Ricky's problems were a result of destructive criticism from his parents. Many parents make the mistake of offering love and approval to their children only when they do what they want them to do or act in a certain way. A child like Ricky, who grew up in an environment where love was conditional, tends to seek unconditional approval throughout their life. When Ricky became an adult, this need for approval seeped into his relationship, placing Anna Marie into the role of a surrogate mother. Dr Roseman (and Feldman), a heart specialist from San Francisco, has defined this desire to have full control over a partner as Type A behaviour, a behaviour associated with jealousy, control, obsession, and attention-seeking. It was clear what poor Anna Marie was going through. It was evident that Ricky's parents had potentially only loved him when he behaved in a manner that they found acceptable. When he was naughty, they withdrew their love, disciplining him whenever he failed to live up to their expectations. If this were the case, it would have sapped his confidence, instilling deep-rooted feelings of worthlessness and inferiority. These feelings would have triggered negative emotions later in life.

Ricky needed a lifeline. He needed to learn how to trust Anna Marie and offer her love that was not conditional on her behaving a certain way. At the end of the process, both Anna Marie and Ricky would emerge as stronger people who were able to show one another complete love in an envelope of trust and respect. Ricky was not able to realise that his childhood experiences were not the best. A child accepts their home environment as it is. Being so young and so inexperienced in life, they do not understand that their personal experience is not necessarily the norm. A child has a natural need to rely on their parents to survive.

Inflict Misery

As a child, it is possible that Ricky had learned that if he misbehaved, he would displease his parents. He understood that his parents could easily withdraw their love should he act in a way they didn't agree with. Of course, most parents don't understand that they are bringing their children up with conditional love. If, on the other hand, Ricky toed the line they had set for him, love was returned to his life, and the anger from his parents subsided. Ricky learned by example, to get angry (or jealous) if things didn't go his way, an understanding that led to his low self-esteem and his desire to inflict misery on his partner. Anna Marie saw the logic behind my presumptions about Ricky's early life and set out to research the best way forward for their relationship. She returned to a later session full of enthusiasm clutching printed examples of case studies describing the behaviour of individuals who suffered from low self-esteem. Like Ricky, these individuals all exhibited traits of anger, jealousy, and lack of trust.

I took the opportunity to meet with Ricky and asked him outright whether he really loved Anna Marie. He proclaimed that he loved her with all his heart; to which I bluntly told him that his behaviour was causing his fiancée a great deal of distress, further asking him where he thought the relationship was heading. With a look of horror, Ricky admitted that he could see their relationship coming to an end if he was unable to change. The end of the relationship would, in his words, be the end of his world. In an attempt to lighten Ricky's load, I explained to him that he had the power to stop that from happening, but the situation was firmly in his hands. Ricky all but begged me to tell how he could prevent his relationship from ending. How could he make his love for Anna Marie a reality forever? Thankfully, unconditional love means that it doesn't matter what you did or said; you are still loved. You can discipline a child but always finish off by telling them how much you love them.

I took the time to explain to Ricky about the emotional impact of conditional love in childhood on adult life and how his early experiences might have brought on low self-esteem which, in turn, had acted as a trigger for his negative behaviours. Ricky was determined to rid himself of this negativity and requested my help in doing so. We discussed self-concept – the beliefs an individual has about themselves. I explained that psychologists had found that many of these beliefs are false and that the only way to rid oneself of these self-limiting beliefs was to concentrate on building high self-esteem using a series of mindful actions. Change would take time and discipline, but if Ricky was determined to save his relationship, that time and discipline were worthy investments.

As I've heard it said – 'Everybody wants the nice things in life, but nobody wants to pay the price.' Ricky assured me that he was willing to pay whatever price was necessary to save his relationship with Anna Marie. Together, Ricky and I went through the series of self-concept building exercises which were to be completed over 21 consecutive days. This would put pathways, or neural grooves, in Ricky's brain and ultimately develop into strong habits that would continue for the rest of his life with Anna Marie. Ricky was emphatic in his assurances that he would keep up the new routine for the next 21 days.

I encouraged Ricky to write down five values and five goals, telling him that the ideas that he came up with must become part of his daily routine. He must also visualise positive images of himself acting more agreeably toward Anna Marie, explaining how to create these visual images in the alpha-theta state.

I explained to Ricky how he must start to use affirmations, both first thing in the morning and throughout each day, using words such as 'I am the best', 'I like myself', 'I can do this', 'I know something wonderful is going to happen to me today'. He must then create a mental video of his new life at least three times each day. These positive statements would start to prepare his mind for positivity. If a negative thought such as jealousy or anger should creep into his mind, he should replace it immediately with a positive thought instead. For example, he could reflect on his goals or a previous success and should nothing come to mind; he could simply say another affirmation.

The Law of Substitution

This is called the Law of Substitution. Users of the method substitute a negative thought with a positive thought. It takes tremendous discipline but with sufficient focus will change a person's thinking.

To ensure Ricky was able to remain in a positive place, I instructed him to stay away from negative people, places, and reading material. He must also introduce exercise into his life, preferably in the mornings straight after repeating his affirmations. This exercise would not only help him to burn calories all day but would also allow oxygen to reach and stimulate his brain. By doing all this for 21 days, new habits would be formed, and he would become a more confident and more loveable person. If Ricky were to work successfully on his inner world and his self-concept, his outer world would become a mirror image. His self-confidence would grow, and he would finally be able to put an end to negative behaviours such as anger, jealousy, and blame.

Unwilling to Pay the Price

After hearing all this, and despite his earlier eagerness to do whatever was required of him, Ricky told me that he couldn't be bothered to 'do all that'. That proved he had no self-discipline. That old saying again, 'Everybody wants the nice things in life, but nobody wants to pay the price.'

Feeling sad, I explained to him that millions of people had been able to conquer their feelings of jealousy and low self-esteem and lead happy and positive lives by using these same techniques. Ricky became very angry and reiterated that I was expecting too much and that there was no way he would be taking my advice. Somewhat flabbergasted, I calmly told Ricky that this is what it would take to save his relationship. He simply became even angrier and stormed out of my office. This was a man who was clearly in his comfort zone and wasn't prepared to do what was necessary to get out of it. He wasn't prepared to pay the price to put his relationship on a better footing, and I began to wonder whether Ricky simply wanted to control his partner and to hell with her feelings.

Of course, Anna Marie was extremely sad to hear the results of my meeting with Ricky. Her fiancée's behaviour was causing her great sadness, but her research had uncovered something that disturbed her far more. Anna Marie had identified that parents with low self-esteem raise children with low self-esteem. How, then, could she marry Ricky and have children knowing the kind of life they were destined to lead. Sadly, she told me that it would be extremely cruel to bring children into an environment where one of their main role models regularly indulged in sulking and arguing. This would become her children's norm. She really did surprise me with her clarity on the situation. Parents have a massive effect on shaping their children's personalities, positive or negative, which usually stays with them for the rest of their lives. This lady had truly looked deeply into the jaws of hell and had not liked what she had seen one bit.

Anna Marie and Ricky's relationship limped on for another two months. Anna Marie spent much of this time pleading with her fiancée to change his mind about attempting to change his behaviour. Was he unwilling to even try to put my advice into practice? Where was his motivation to improve their relationship? She told him repeatedly that she loved him, but she needed him to give the 21-day process a go for both of their sakes. Alas, Ricky was adamant that he would not make the effort required for him to change, and his negative behaviour continued at its same destructive pace. Ricky's negativity had triggered deep mechanical thinking. The person won't change but simply stays in their comfort zone, resisting change, and failing to take any responsibility for a situation.

I can still recall the day that Anna Marie phoned me out of the blue to tell me that she still loved Ricky, but she now understood that his behaviour would not change. She had left him.

In a way, Aristotle, the Greek philosopher, was proved right. He called Ricky's activity the Law of Causality. It changed Western thinking to the way it is today, although it is now known as the Law of Cause and Effect. For every effect you have in your life, there is always a cause. The effect on Ricky's life was that Anna Marie had left him. The cause was his controlling, jealous, and demanding behaviour.

Ricky, of course, was unable to accept the situation, so it came as little surprise that he came to see me, pleading with me to ask Anna Marie to go back to him. He was simply furious that she had not given him her new address and I was, of course, unwilling to furnish him with the information. Instead, I told Ricky that Anna Marie still loved him but, if he wanted one last chance at the relationship, the onus was on him to commit to making the necessary changes. While Ricky was insistent that he loved Anna Marie, it was clear that he was only willing to offer that love on his terms. His unabated need to control his partner was demonstrated by the aggression he showed when insisting that he did not need to change.

This is a typical example of mechanical thinking, and it left me quite sad that things had turned out this way for Anna Marie and Ricky. I was angry with myself that I had been unable to persuade Ricky to make changes for just 21 days. My own mentor told me that it was near impossible for Ricky to change, likening the situation to trying to teach a pig to fly. Firstly, a pig can never fly. Secondly, it will only become angrier when you continue to try to teach it to fly. So, what's the point of trying to teach a pig to fly? It will never happen.

Broken Heart

I kept in touch with Anna Marie and hoped to see her do well in life. For a while, she remained sad, haunted by her lost love and what could have been under different circumstances. She did feel that Ricky loved her, but it broke her heart that he wasn't willing to make the changes needed to ensure that they and any future children could enjoy a happy life.

Another six months later, Ricky had found another young lady. He was able to control this girl, and his old behaviour patterns continued. It's been told that this poor girl probably didn't have the courage to stand up to Ricky. It's possible they got married and had kids, bringing them up in an environment that Anna Marie had managed to avoid. Anna Marie's new path was to lead her to meet a man with high self-esteem. They are now happily married with two beautiful, well-adjusted children. She feels very fortunate to have met her new partner.

I am reminded of a quote by Benjamin Disraeli. He said, 'No success in public life can compensate for failure in the home.' Anna Marie realised that her personal life should take precedence over everything else. That's why she left Ricky, closed her business, and moved away. She used the Law of Attraction which states that you will attract into your life the kind of person who is very much the way you are, a person just like her new husband who had the same beliefs and values as her and the same goal of raising self-confident children with high self-esteem. And, of course, she had high self-esteem herself, unlike 'never teach a pig to fly' Ricky.

What Anna Marie had experienced is so typical of many broken relationships. Stephen Covey, writing in *The Seven Habits of Highly Effective People*, said, 'Before you climb the ladder of success, make sure it is leaning on the right building.' This is true in business but also in relationships and marriage too. There is only one route to long-term happiness and finding your soulmate.

Let's look into finding the right relationship and your soulmate.

How to determine if your relationship is going in the right direction:

1. Like attracts Like

The Law of Attraction states that you mix in harmony with those people who share the same attributes as you. Birds of a feather flock together. Are your partner's beliefs the same as yours? Do you share the same characteristics such as; honesty, integrity, kindness, and pride? Do you have similar goals for education, health, and family life? You will always be at your happiest with a partner who has similar interests, tastes, and values to your own. It's great if you have the same attitude towards money – how it is earned, how it is saved, and how it is spent. Partners should also have the same attitude toward children – whether to have them, how many to have, and how to raise them.

Stupid Ricky lost Anna Marie because he didn't want to learn all this. He was more interested in controlling her. Further attitudes which should be shared are feelings about sex, social issues, politics, spirituality, and how to spend leisure time. Most unhappiness in relationships come down to fundamental disagreements about these basic issues.

2. Communication

Nature demands balance and harmony. There should be a free flow of conversation between you and your partner. Neither should try to dominate the relationship. Communication should be equal. Neither of you should do all the talking and rarely let the other to get a word in edgeways. Communication should be balanced. Test your relationship on a long car journey without the radio playing. Is there a free flow of conversation, with both actively listening to each other? Are silences awkward or comfortable? A couple with the same interests, hobbies, and values are likely to communicate easily, with each party benefitting from 50% airtime. In other words, they are respectful and interested in what their partner has to say. The main reason for the success of a relationship is that the two people communicate well with each other. They are on the same wavelength. They seem to understand what the other person is feeling, almost like they share a brain. On the other hand, poor communication can result in the failure of a relationship. The couple misunderstands each other and continually argue about issues, large and small, each convinced that they are right, and their partner is wrong. The most important question in an argument is to ask yourself 'what is important here?' – Winning the argument or maintaining the quality of your relationship. Practice the golden rule of relationships – ask yourself 'what would it be like to be married to me?' and 'what would it be like if my partner treated me the way I treat them?' Life is a study of attention. If you pay attention to the small things in your relationships, the big things will typically take care of themselves. Always endeavour to be a loving and thoughtful communicator in your relationships.

3. Commitment

Total commitment requires heartfelt determination to make the relationship successful. It means that neither partner should ever consider separating, breaking up, or divorcing. In total commitment, you burn all physical and emotional bridges. People like Ricky avoid making a total commitment because they have been hurt in other relationships but as W. Scott Peck said in his book The Road Less Travelled – 'Love is the total commitment to the full development of the potential of the other'. I have read that relationship experts have found that if one partner fails to give 100% commitment, the relationship will flounder. Some men want to carry on as if they were still single, by going out with the boys and drinking too much, thus forgetting their family. Being married demands a great deal of commitment to each other; otherwise, there is a risk that one or both partners will end up hurt. Today, couples across the world often take out a prenuptial agreement, ensuring that, if there is an irreconcilable breakdown, there will be a positive financial outcome. Is that total commitment? In a loving relationship, it is essential to love, respect, and take account of the needs and wishes of the other person. Now that's commitment.

4. The Best Friend Test:

I have read that often; it is important that two people are good friends before starting a serious relationship. Friendship is the glue that binds a relationship together. Couples who have been happily married for years say that this is because a great friendship has allowed their love to blossom. Even if their relationship were to break down, they would remain friends for life. This is especially important if children are involved. In the ideal relationship, your partner will be your best friend. There would be no one else that you would sooner spend time with. If you don't feel that way, then something is seriously wrong. In a long-term relationship, people fall in and out of love – as the intensity of their feelings changes over time. If those two people in a long-term relationship continue to like and respect each other at times when the love isn't so strong, their relationship will survive regardless. Sometimes, relationships and marriages don't work out, but if the partnership was initially based on liking and respecting each other, the two people can usually continue to communicate at an adult level.

Out of curiosity, I want you to give some thought to your answers to these questions.

First, may I ask you that when you have a serious problem to whom do you confide? Is it your parents, a work colleague, a best friend, an old school friend or a sibling? Is it your partner?

Who do you laugh with and share the same sense of humour with? Couples who laugh together, stay together. Do you laugh with your partner?

When you hear a secret or of a secret, who is the first person you want to share it with. After all, a secret is only a secret if you share it with one person at a time. Do you share a secret with your partner?

When you receive some special news, who is the first person you want to celebrate with? Is it your partner? Your best friend?

Be honest with your answers to gain insight into your relationship.

There are many reasons why relationships break down, and so much heartache is caused, but I have read that you can boil it down to six major problems – and these are what Ricky and Anne Marie were facing. These are the root cause of arguments, disagreement, anger, jealousy, and divorce. Lots of relationships have them, just like Ricky's were caused by low self-esteem, low self-confidence, and a poor self-image. So, let's learn from, in my opinion, and experience, other people's mistakes and not try to reinvent the wheel. Please don't do what failures do!

5. Happiness or misery?

The Law of Suggestology states that 95% of our feelings are a result of outside sources.

How to apply the test? If you wake up on a cold and wet Monday morning, how do you feel after you heard bad news on the radio or television? Do you understand that these negative events influence your emotional brain? Your brain feeds on both negative and positive thoughts and, with mental strength, can cope with the negativity. In other words, your brain is like a chameleon, ever-changing. This can be applied to any relationship. If one person in a relationship has a happy-go-lucky personality and the other is unhappy as a result of being raised in a negative environment, such as one of conditional love, the less happy person will likely have a negative impact on the happier partner. It is the power of 'suggestology' that indicates this is likely to happen. However, if the person is strong-willed, there is a possibility that the unhappy person will take on the happy and positive behaviours. Show the world a happy smiling face and a positive outlook.

The daughter of a friend once evidenced an example of this to me. She was a very positive, friendly, and outgoing person with a smile for everyone. Everything about her showed that she had been part of a happy family, who gave her complete unconditional love. I happened to meet her and her new husband in later life, only to find that she had completely changed. The sparkle in her eyes had gone, and her positive attitude was no more. Alas, she had married a miserable, pessimistic, and moody man who had negatively influenced her outlook on life. The chameleon had won again.

She knew she was unhappy and, one morning decided that she could no longer live with her miserable husband and filed for divorce, taking her one and only child with her. Fortunately, Anna Marie did not have to go through all the suffering that divorce brings with it by leaving Ricky before it was too late.

So, it is massively important for people to be in the right relationship, for their ladder to be leaning against the right building, and to be in a loving, happy situation with unconditional love and happy demeanour. This accords with the saying 'fly with the eagle, don't scratch with turkeys'.

6. Are you on the same wavelength?

Simply putting it, do you and your partner have some shared interests, and do you agree on important issues? Don't get me wrong – it's important for people to have their own opinions and points of view but it is important to be ready to give your partner a walkover and let them win because you love them so much. It is important to recognise when you are wrong, own up to the fact, and apologise. On reflection, would it not be a great idea if political leaders around the world were honest enough to admit their mistakes and apologise wholeheartedly, taking responsibility? This would show true honesty and integrity and win respect from their constituents.

I'm sure it was Richard Branson that said, 'The sign of a great leader is sometimes to say, sorry, I made a mistake, I was wrong'. They thought that they had it right, but they realise they were totally incorrect; if you can admit that in your relationships, your life will change forever.

When you take the ability to say sorry into personal relationships, it enables better understanding, direct lines of communication, and open-mindedness. This is the exact opposite of Ricky's philosophy – he was always right regardless of the situation.

Are you and your partner seeing things through each other's eyes? Are you on the same wavelength or are you poles apart? Be honest and score yourself from 1 to 10. (1 being that you aren't, and 10 being totally in sync).

7. Look at yourself!

So far, we have looked at your partner. Do not forget to look at yourself and try to assess what it would be like to be married to you! Self-knowledge will give you an insight into how others see you. You are either in for a nasty shock or a pleasant surprise. Having established what the result is, you know what you must do.

Anna Marie was able to look objectively at her situation and come to a logical and reasoned decision, taking into account the following:

> A. Jealousy really is the green-eyed monster. As we need to realise that if we are being jealous or making others jealous; we are exhibiting low self-esteem and low self-worth.
>
> B. Pity. Woe is me. The world owes me a living. Nobody has it worse than me. In this way, we are acting with the mentality of a child.
>
> C. Negativity. Expectations or lack thereof. It's not what you want in life; it's what you expect. Weak people expect the worst.
>
> D. Laughter has dried up. The brain has a dimmer switch. When there is no fun and

laughter in a relationship, the light darkens until it goes out completely.

E. Pre-occupied with own interests and/or work. A lack of work/life balance with all the focus on work is a sure disaster for relationships.

If you now really want to save your relationship, work your socks off to put love back into it. Ask your partner to go through the love test. If they are hostile to the idea, they may not be the person you hope they are.

1. Ask him or her or act and feel as if you are courting again. Giggle, smile, and look into each other's eyes. Do this for 21 days. The brain will form all the neural pathways, and new habits will be established.
2. Look for admirable qualities in one another — praise and offer compliments at every opportunity.
3. Give attention and actively listen for even a small comment and reiterate it. Remember that imitation is the sincerest form of flattery. Do the things you did when you fell in love.
4. Forgive and forget mistakes and misunderstandings. After all, wrong assumptions are the number one reason for failure in any situation.
5. Just keep your mind on the attributes you love about the other person.
6. Get into the habit of giving small compliments and then adding the words 'I really do love you'.

If you and your partner can do this for 21 days, you will notice a remarkable change in your attitude and relationship. If there are children, you can do the same with them. To do this, you must be prepared to take on the greatest fight of your life. This is your time. Make sure it is filled with love for and from your soulmate.

The lovely Anna Marie is so happy with her beautiful children because she really did take the time to find the love of her life, someone who could give her unconditional love and room to express herself within a loving and caring relationship.

Reflection is Wisdom

The second rule of the love test is…?

The third rule of the love test is commitment. What are you showing in a relationship when you don't burn your bridges? Give three examples.

The fourth rule for a best friend test. Give examples of situations that confirm you have found your best friend.

The fifth rule is happiness or misery? What do you think about the happy or miserable chameleon?

The sixth rule is, are you on the same wavelength? Give three examples.

The warning signs of a stretched relationship are jealousy, self-pity, low self-esteem, blame and anger.

Can you identify anyone else who is facing these challenges?

How do you put the love back into a relationship?

Do the same things when you were _____?
Attention is _____?
Catch your partner doing things right_____?
Praise _____ and_____?
See it through their _____?
Forgive and _____?

Wrong Assumptions Are the Root of All Misunderstandings.

They are, in fact, planning for the separation. It makes one partner feel that they are not good enough if there is no full commitment. Then it brings the feeling of being rejected.

In all relationships, the only way is to commit yourself deeply and give 100%. From now on, offer 100% commitment in every relationship. Your job differently. Your future. No prenuptial agreement.

The 'wrong ladder up against the wrong building' or, as we say, the partner is not the right one; I used always to find when I was younger that I was jealous, when my confidence and self-esteem were low, that's when the green-eyed monster came out. I have to think it was because I was going through destructive criticism at my job at the time. I began to feel that nobody could ever love me. Years later, I realised that my jealousy had nothing to do with the other person. It was just my low self-esteem. I pledged that I would never ever make another person jealous.

Your inner world reflects your outer world. We can change on the outside. But we never try to change on the inside. Still that funny laugh, still up and down mood swings, still the same. This time next year, we could be millionaires and sadly have all the same habits and negativity because of low self-esteem and taking offence easily.

So, what you see is what you get. If the other partner accepts that and looks for the good qualities of their partner and encourages and praises their natural talents, then and only then will the partnership become more stable. So, go with confident expectations with your loved ones from now on.

The next wrong ladder in relationships is a lack of commitment. Sometimes in relationships, people don't like to burn their bridges. For any relationship to work, it has to be based on full commitment from both sides. As soon as one partner only goes 49%, then a split starts. And as I have found at times in my own turbulent life, then the other partner only gives 47% then 40% then 30%, until he or she stops trying at all.

Happiness

The key to happiness is often said to be finding our soulmate and living happily ever after. It sounds easy but often proves trickier in real life. The reason a good relationship is hard to come by – or can become one of the best relationships of your life - is expectations. It's not what you *want* from life but what you *expect.* It is the first rung of the relationships ladder.

Past experiences often lead people to expect the worst of people, and these expectations can fall hard on their partner's shoulders. They anticipate that their partner will be late, forget to pick up the groceries or take six months to get around to doing a minor repair job in the home. These negative expectations can become a self-fulfilling prophecy, slowly wearing away at the will and determination of their partner to make a good go of things. With their other half expecting, and in some cases, willing them to fail, and continually reminding them of their mistakes, these downtrodden partners are under an immense amount of pressure. These couples may still love each other dearly, but the cracks begin to show under the weight of the constant pressure from one side of the relationship. However, if the person with negative expectations can somehow manage instead to focus on positive expectations, then the situation becomes a great deal different, and the resulting relationship can be joyful. By flipping expectation of a partner always falling short to believing that they will do the right thing and making them aware of your confidence in them by using phrases such as; 'I know you will get on brilliantly with my mother,' or, 'Thanks so much for agreeing to pick up the groceries tonight,' or, 'Have a great night with your friends and I'll see you around 10 pm when you get home.' Those previously underestimated partners become empowered to meet your positive expectations.

The next rung of the ladder is 'I will change you.' You've probably heard people telling you that you need to change multiple times throughout your life so far. You may have even heard an engaged woman vow to change the less desirable habits of her soon-to-be husband after they get married. The thing is that change rarely occurs. It's a fact of life that people never really change. You must have heard the old saying that a leopard never really changes its spots. It turns out that most humans don't either. By the age of 16, past thoughts and experiences, negative and positive expectations from others and our good and bad habits mean that our personalities are very much formed and, in many cases, are set as hard as concrete. We are so set in our ways that when we are told we must change or when a partner vows to make the changes for us, the expected changes very rarely take place. School reunions are a great example of this.

Parenthood

After 18 months of marriage, my wife and I experienced the great joy of the arrival of a child, a daughter who we named Joanne. I only wish that I had been educated enough to bring up my daughter in the right way. Alas, parenthood is a master skill and one that can rarely be taught in advance. As parents, we rely heavily on our instincts and from our past experiences of watching the parenting technique of others, good or bad. There is no honours degree in parenting. You must simply get on with the job. I soon became to understand that when you bring a child into the world, it is a job like no other- relationships, both friendly and romantic, come and go, we change our roles in work, sometimes earning more money than before, we move to a new house – but parenting is a role for life. Once we become a parent, that doesn't change. We are a parent until the day we die. Parenthood is one of the most profound responsibilities that any adult can shoulder and a role in which we all begin as amateurs. It is our job to raise our children to have a deep sense of self-confidence and self-respect. Our children should feel great about themselves, about who they are, what they have achieved, and what they might achieve in the future. I desperately wanted to be an excellent parent to Joanne, a parent whom she could look up and respect, a role model if you like. I'm ashamed to say that I failed Joanne, through little more than sheer ignorance.

Love Yourself, Then You Can Love Your Children

I can identify two reasons why I failed her. The first one being, as I said before, that like millions of other parents, I had low self-esteem. I struggled to give more love to Joanne that I had for myself. The second being that the friction between parents and their children is the feeling or perception of parents that their children are failing to measure up to what their parents expect them to be or do. Many parents look upon their children as a form of property, feeling like I did that their children are only behaving properly when they are doing or saying things according to their parent's expectations. The parents respond with criticism. I did that, and I hate myself for doing it. I once read that children are not your property; your children belong to themselves. They are simply a gift to you from high above – and a temporary gift at that. If only I had realised that my daughter was a precious gift that I could only enjoy for a short time. If only I had understood that I was a role model for my child so that I could behave differently. I sometimes blamed and criticised her for behaving in a certain way, failing to realise that I was the primary source of that behaviour. It is true to say that the apple never falls far from the tree. Children fill their emotional tank from drinking in love from their parents. They are like a rose. When the sun shines, and the rain falls, the rose blooms and grows. If there is no sun and rain, the rose with wither and die, so be sure to give your child the sun of love and the rain of growth every day. Give them continual love, praise and encouragement every day. Hugs and kisses are a great way to convey to your children that you love them.

I read about a family therapist that said children require four hugs a day for survival, eight hugs a day for health and 12 hugs a day for growth. There is so much more we could all do to raise happy, healthy, and confident children. I had thought I was doing a good job, but hindsight makes me realise that my low self-esteem prevented me from being a great dad. I'm sorry, Joanne.

So, I believe the most important skill in the world is developing happy children with high self-esteem.

'If you fly with eagles you will always find your soulmate.'

Let's reflect on what you have just learnt.

1. What caused Anna Marie to be upset and alarmed by Ricky's behaviour?
2. What were Ricky's four behaviour patterns?
3. Where was Anna Marie when she caught Ricky spying on her?
4. Why had Ricky formed negative behaviour patterns?
5. What are the action points of the 21-day habit-forming process?
6. What gives you the most happiness in life? Finding your...?
7. What are all the three parts of hugs?
8. What is the key to parenthood?
9. What does a negative chameleon do to you?

'For true love is inexhaustible; the more you give, the more you have. And if you go to draw at the true fountainhead, the more water you draw, the more abundant is its flow.' Antoine De Saint-Exupery.

6. THE SORROW OF LOSING TIME

'To achieve a goal you've never achieved before, you are going to have to develop and master a skill you've never had before.' Brian Tracy.

Reflection

As I went through my life, learning and growing from my days at Hygena, after leaving school when I was 14½, I started educating myself, and not wasting any more of my time.

When asking people aged over 85 about their greatest regrets, numerous surveys reveal that the overriding source of remorse for the so-called fourth generation is that they had wasted their precious times and lost years. When asked to elaborate, these people describe how they wasted time working in the wrong job and hanging out with the wrong people. Respondents report that they spent these years in denial, feeling that it was perhaps better to maintain the status quo and simply hope things would improve. These improvements almost never materialised, leaving many people feeling that, if they had their time again, they would have gone with their gut feeling - the small voice from within - and made difficult but courageous decisions to leave the partners they no longer loved, seek the changes they desired in their work and kick non-supportive friends to the kerb. The absence of these courageous decisions left survey respondents living with an element of sorrow.

Time is Our Most Precious Resource

Delving deeper into the mindset of octogenarians reveals an additional set of regrets. For some, it is regret concerning the boring neighbourhood they lived in. For others, it is the time spent watching TV and browsing trashy magazines instead of taking up interesting hobbies, reading self-help books, and meeting worthwhile new friends. While these people had been unsatisfied with certain areas of their lives, they had also been concerned about the drawbacks of change and had made an unconscious decision to stick with their bad habits and stay within their comfort zone. These findings should act as a warning. The clock is ticking for us all and to not take steps to reduce the risk of facing similar regrets in our old age is nothing short of a wasted opportunity. While the fourth generation may not be in a position to benefit from change at this point in their lives, they may perhaps feel better if they knew that a younger generation could learn from their negative experiences.

Take a moment to consider the world's most important resource. Does your mind turn to thoughts of money, to bricks and mortar or sparkling gems? These resources are by no means unimportant but pale in comparison to that of time. Time is our most precious resource.

Once lost, time can never be reclaimed. With courage, you can succeed in a new job following redundancy or find love with a new partner after a breakup. You can start over in many areas of life but never with time. So why, then, do people continue to waste the most precious of the world's resources? Why do they argue with their family or choose to work late each night and, in the process, miss their children growing up? Why do they spend time with negative people and on unfulfilling activities? Would it not be better that they devote their lives to learning new skills, enjoying quality time with valued friends and family or to empowering the sick and poor to enjoy a more satisfying life?

The psychology of time management is a critical skill and one which, when mastered, will have an enormous effect on both your business and personal life. My own understanding of the importance of effective time management came when my daughter Joanne turned 16 – one minute she was five, then one day she said 'Dad.' And I turned around and there she was 16! I was devastated, because of work, I had missed the best years of her life.

It had seemed but a moment earlier that she had been a toddler. Having asked myself the searching question of where those years had gone, I came to the uncomfortable realisation that I had missed my daughter's childhood in favour of channelling all my energy into climbing the career ladder. I was the dad who never saw his child's Christmas play, and the dad who didn't have time to play with his daughter after school. Put simply; I was the dad who was too busy. In my race to reach the top in my career, which brought with it many years of worrying, I had lost out on what are arguably the best years of parenthood.

The 80/20 Rule

I was devastated and resolved immediately to make a change in my life - determined to not miss out for a minute longer, to say to hell with that job that took up so much of my precious time and to finally learn the art and the psychology of time management. Having failed so spectacularly in earlier efforts, I decided to seek the help of an expert - someone who could help me to understand why I spent so much time at work yet failed to see any real benefits from my efforts. This decision was one that would change my life.

I took part in many soul-searching sessions with my mentor but not before he analysed my typical daily routine. His immediate conclusion was that I was violating the Pareto Principle (more commonly known as the 80/20 rule or the law of the vital few versus the trivial many). This principle advocates that 80 per cent of results come from 20 per cent of effort. Conversely, 80 per cent of your activities can often lead to just 20 per cent of your successes.

Clearly, spending so much time to achieve so few of your results is not the most efficient way to live. Yet, that is exactly how I spent so many years of my life. I had wasted years of my precious time slogging away for 14 hours every day, had brought work home with me much of the time and, most devastatingly of all, had missed my child grow up. And for what? Had I risen to the very top of the company where I had spent long years toiling away? Had I accomplished more than the average job? Had my results been so bloody spectacular that I was respected far and wide in my field? Not a chance. My time had been poorly spent, my life, to that point at least, had been a waste of time, and my overall results were mediocre at best. Enough was enough. A combination of my own disappointment and the enlightening yet encouraging words from my mentor had convinced me that a change must take place.

Action Oriented

I decided to organise my life, so that I could get more done faster, in a shorter period of time. I was told that the more alert you are, the more likely it is that you will be aware of opportunities and situations that you can turn to your advantage. Many people's lives have changed by spotting, and listening to, top people and identifying new trends in the marketplace. So, I was always on alert to save time, so I could see my family more. and have time for my education.

Momentum

Sir Isaac Newton said, 'A person in motion tends to remain in motion, it takes less energy to keep moving than it does to start moving again.'
It was why I was always so tired at night when I got home.
I was always stopping and starting.
I learned that you require ten units of energy to get you moving initially, but you need only two units of energy to keep you moving. This was my problem if I stopped for any reason; it would take another ten units of energy to get going once more. Stupid me, I was always going to see my poor doctor and asking him why was tired all the time.
So, from then on, I became a moving target; I kept in motion.

Years later, I witnessed lots of people stopping and starting and some people who stopped never got going again.

Are Your Plates Spinning?

The good news is, the faster you move, the more you get done. The faster you move, the more likely you do the right thing for the right person at the right time. Keep the plates spinning in your life like a circus performer, keep applying pressure on the stick so that the plates are spinning indefinitely. As you know, if the plates slow down all the plates will fall off. And my plates up till then were always falling off. Please, please, don't let this happen to you; keep your energy, and you will find just by using two units of energy all day you will create more time for the people you love.

No Productive Meetings

Sessions with my mentor quickly revealed that I was spending around 50 per cent of my time simply attending meetings and networking events. Never was this so apparent than when looking at the example of the monthly meetings called by my finance director at the time. These events involved so much travel that a few hours spent in a meeting could easily turn into over a day and a half of lost productivity for all ten attendees. The next time I was summoned to one of these time-wasting events, my mentor instructed me to ring the finance director to inquire whether an agenda was available, and whether it was necessary for me to attend. It's fair to say that these questions went down like a proverbial lead balloon. I was basically told that I was playing games and my job would be on the line if I turned out to be a no-show at this terribly important meeting.

Do you think that stopped me? Hell no! It wasn't too difficult to identify that the finance director's hotspot was money. He was, after all, always talking about how the company was losing it everywhere he looked. I decided to present him with some eye-opening information and set about calculating the true cost of each of these meetings by adding together the average hourly salary of attendees, the travelling costs and the subsequent overtime payments made to staff who had no choice but to catch up on their work out of regular hours. This added up to a pretty penny, especially when considering the annual cost. Better still is that it was the finance director who continually bemoaned the fact that the company was losing money that was signing off on this excessive and wholly unnecessary expenditure. He didn't mince his words by calling me a 'little shit' when presented with this information but did call a halt to the meetings unless they were deemed imperative. I became something of a hero among my colleagues, but of more importance to me was that I now found myself with a little more time to spend with my family.

The idea that you might waste time in meetings is probably nothing new. Top business outlets such as HubSpot, Fast Company and Management Today have all suggested similar - with some research indicating that up to 70 per cent of your time at work is wasted. You, yourself, have likely been in a fair few meetings that are a complete waste of time. Perhaps you even know some people who love meetings simply for the fact that they can sit there for hours while drinking the coffee, eating the biscuits, and contributing very little at all. Don't be that person. Don't be the one to waste your life in snooze mode at pointless meeting after pointless meeting. Don't be the person who finds themselves taking work home every night at the expense of family time. In short, don't be the me that I once was.

Having identified just how much time I was wasting in meetings - and believe me when I say that the finance director's monthly event was just the beginning - my mentor showed me a simple way out by explaining that every time I was asked to attend a meeting, I should ask the following questions before accepting the request:

1. Why do I have to attend the meeting?
2. What is the purpose of the meeting?
3. What results will I get from attending?

4. Is the meeting truly necessary?

These simple questions helped me to respond to meeting requests in a different and infinitely more productive way, and I soon found that I had more time on my hands due to banishing many of these time sucks from my working life. But what if you're the one requesting the meeting? There's nothing quite like the feeling of satisfaction you get from showing others how it's done. You need to walk the walk, so to speak. My mentor offered me seven tips to help me streamline my meetings and get results. I've used them consistently since then to great effect, and now you can too.

1. Whether you're planning a meeting with your boss, your colleagues, or a single client, having a pre-defined agenda is critical. Without one, you'll find that your meetings overrun and you likely won't even cover the most important issues. Your agenda should start with a clear statement of the purpose of the meeting, followed by a list of all items to be discussed. You should distribute your agenda 24 hours before the meeting, thus allowing attendees to be fully prepared. Personal experience tells me that people love the clarity that this approach offers them.

2. You should always start and end your meeting at the published time. There's nothing more frustrating than waiting for people who are late or as disheartening as a meeting that goes on and on with no end in sight. Of course, being as determined as I was, I took things one step further by locking the door on latecomers. Trust me when I say that those people were so embarrassed by the time I eventually let them in, that they showed up on time after that.

3. By finishing on time, you show respect for your col-

leagues' busy schedules.

4. Remember the Pareto Principle? The 80/20 rule can be easily applied to meetings. Let's say you had ten things you wanted to discuss. You should identify the top two things that you can't afford to miss and get them out the way first. That way, if you run out of time and must close the meeting, the only things left are the less important details that can either be discussed at your next event or agreed over the phone or by email.

5. Summarise each section of the agenda as you progress. By providing a quick summary at the end of each section, you provide additional clarity to attendees and ensure that everyone leaves on the same page. That summary is also a great time to confirm who has been actioned with specific responsibilities, so you should include names, tasks, and time frames in that overview. Each summary is also a great time to let attendees who are no longer needed leave the meeting and get on with their day.

6. Having a record of your meeting is essential although you won't want feverish notetaking to get in the way of your discussions flowing smoothly. For this reason, it's crucial that you learn the art of mind mapping. From your mind maps, you should create a set of brief notes to circulate to attendees confirming what has been discussed and what actions have been agreed.

7. If appropriate, include crisis anticipation in your meetings. Things go wrong; that's life! It's how you deal with unexpected setbacks that matters. It's important that you take some time to consider what could go wrong with your plans and identify what actions can be taken. By agreeing on these actions in advance, you reduce the risk of panic and blame-setting in and avoid having to have yet more

meetings to decide what to do on the fly. Make your motto to prepare and not simply react.

8. Join the standing up revolution. You've likely heard about the new health trend inspiring office workers across the globe to stand, rather than sit at their desks, while typing away. As it turns out, this approach can be used to great effect in meetings too. Jack Welch, the long-time CEO of General Electric, was an avid fan of having everyone stand up at meetings, using the technique to ensure his meetings were quick, to the point and got results.

Using these tips helped me to gain a name for myself quickly - for holding great meetings. There's no reason they can't work for you too. The only thing standing in your way of a change for the better is you. It's a sobering thought but one which you must accept if you want to succeed.

Decisions, Decisions, Decisions

It wasn't just meetings that were taking up so much of my time and keeping me from enjoying a rewarding family life. Discussions also revealed that my distaste for making decisions, for fear of making a mistake, was also proving problematic. A few stern words from my mentor were all it took to convince me that the ability to make a good decision quickly is one of the keys to effective leadership. My fear of making the wrong decision had become a real problem, but it was not a problem that I faced alone. All around us, although particularly in the council and political landscape, there are people whose constant delays and unyielding procrastination are causing mayhem, not only in their own lives but also in their respective organisations where much time and money are lost. Put simply, holding a position of authority demands that you make timely decisions and stick to them until facts indicate you should take another path.

Constant Change

The guidance offered by my mentor enabled me to see that a significant majority of decisions that are made turn out to be wrong, given the fullness of the time. That doesn't mean that you shouldn't have made the decision in the first place, so long as you did so with your best understanding of the situation at the time. The world around us is in a state of constant transition. People change, knowledge changes and technology changes; all of which can mean that a decision you made in good faith may not have been the best decision. To avoid wasting time and energy, it is important that you made it, nonetheless. Decisions can always be changed in favour of a better course, but you will never find that better course had you not banished procrastination, made your decision based on the facts available at the time and moved forward in the first place.

Overcoming my dislike of decision making was surprisingly simple thanks, of course, to the expert support of my mentor. And just like the new meeting strategies you have now learned; you can also benefit from his knowledge. The next time you have a problem and need to make a decision, use the following steps as a guideline. You'll soon find that you make decisions quickly and are able to move in the right direction.

1. Start by writing the problem down. A clear definition of what your decision relates to is imperative and helps to clear your mind.
2. Avoid Chinese whispers and uncover the facts for yourself. Dig as deep as you can to reveal the true nature and details of the problem.
3. Examine the cause of the problem. Not doing so will cause chaos down the line as without first dealing with the problem before implementing a solution, the problem will likely recur.
4. List 20 possible solutions by having a brain-storming session and choose the best solution after con-

sidering the best and worst possible outcomes for each idea.

5. Remember that all decisions are based on emotion - the emotion of fear and the emotion of gain. Embrace this as you make your decision and never let it prevent you from acting.

It's also worth taking the time to take the test below.

A Time Management Test

Answer the following questions about the different areas of your life. Be honest with yourself - see the situation for how it is and not how you would like it to be in an ideal world. Answer 'Yes' or 'No'. Should you find your answers are mainly 'Yes', it is likely that you are heading the same direction that I once faced myself. When I answered similar questions and finally realised how much time I had wasted, it was enough to bring tears to my eyes.

1. Do you often take work home with you?
2. Do you avoid family time after work, perhaps choosing to watch TV instead?
3. Are you mentally tired and feel that you hate your job?
4. Do you spend significant amounts of personal time thinking about your work?
5. Do you continually find fault with family members?
6. Do you clock watch all day when at work?
7. Do you approach your work slowly and haphazardly?
8. Do you experience Monday morning blues and long for the weekend to arrive?
9. Do you run out of the office door at 5 pm like a fire alarm has just sounded?
10. Do you spend time wondering why you have never been promoted?

11. Do you spend time dreaming about a lottery win?
12. Do you feel envious of people in your company who earn more than you?
13. Do you fail to make significant and regular contributions to your savings?
14. Do you avoid early morning exercise, promising yourself that you will do it later?
15. Do you get so busy throughout the day that you resort to eating junk food?
16. Do you avoid learning opportunities such as courses and self-help books?
17. Do you spend personal time with people you don't really like or appreciate?
18. Do you say yes to demands without considering your existing workload?
19. Do you avoid setting and working toward clearly defined goals?

If you love your family and want to spend more time with them then start being a trader of time; trade your time for knowledge and skills, trade your time with positive people and role models, trade your time on planning your future. And, definitely trade your time to leave a great legacy for your family, and for your life goals. Or, you could trade your time being negative and gossiping, or even trade your time watching television every night. It's your choice; don't make the same mistakes as John Haynes in his early days; time is our most precious resource. Become an excellent trader of time.
'You're flying with the eagles, to be a trader of time.'

Let's put this knowledge into your long-term memory:

1. Procrastination is the thief of _____?
2. Time is our most _____?
3. How many years had I lost with my daughter over my bad time management?
4. How many units of energy do you need to get going

every day?

5. How many units of energy to keep going all day?
6. What was the saying from Sir Isaac Newton?
7. How do you set agendas for meetings?
8. How do you solve problems with the right and left brain?
9. Why should you keep emotions out of decision making?
10. Explain the 80/20 rule!

'Continuous, unflagging effort, persistence and determination will win. Let not the man be discouraged who has these.' James Whitcomb Riley.

7. EVERYTHING HAPPENS FOR A REASON

'If your actions inspire others to dream more, learn more, do more, and become more, then you are a leader.' —John Quincy Adams.

L ooking back now at events; the meeting with my comrades and workmates at Hygena, and all my caring mentors since, knowing what I now know, I realise that this was all part of the universe making my life change for the better. I was on a sharp learning curve. People call this serendipity, everything happens for a reason, and that was the reason that I was having hard, uncertain times all through my life.

Mental Preparation

Let me explain. They say that there are no coincidences in life, some people believe in coincidence, they believe the power of random events shapes a person's life, and that was the way that I went through life, but the fact is that in most cases, coincidences just don't happen. They can always be traced back to previous events and mental preparation, I've always believed in visualisation after my mentor helped me develop it. But rather than coincidence that they are instead a variety of different probabilities that particular events will occur, according to the law of averages; I have always believed this, since being educated about it (of course).

I remember every time I got a door slammed in my face; when I was selling life insurance to the hard-working people of Bootle. I was told it was a numbers game, and if you keep on knocking on people's doors, then it's almost certain somebody will say yes, and buy your product. That's the law of averages if you try enough different things – which is what I was doing during my hard-working life. Like meeting people; people who were rude and unkind to me, like the snotty-nosed interviewers at the unemployment exchange who sniggered at me when they found out I left school when I was 14½ and had received no education since.

But I realise now; I was meeting different people, who could make a difference in my life good or bad.

It's just like billiard balls rolling around the table; one or two of them are going to bang into each other. This coming together of different events is based on the Law of Success or the Law of Coincidences, which are two different principles that I believe in.

I was like one of those billiard balls, meeting hurtful negative people, following failure habits and always blaming everybody for my life mistakes.

But then the billiards balls, with help with the Law of Serendipity, changed my destiny, and I met people who inspired me to take full responsibility for my future.

These principles can be seen throughout the history of humankind; the most successful men and women experience them regularly. Now I'm going to ask you, "Have you ever experienced any of these?" Did something happen to you that really shocked or hurt you?

Looking back, you realise it was a blessing in disguise, and even a great learning curve; even when I was telling my close work friends from the Hygena factory that we were all being made redundant, although for some it was the end of their lives and livelihoods.

Looking back now, I realise that made me stronger and a more astute person; it built my resolve for the years ahead. If I hadn't been made redundant, I wouldn't have gone on to travel the world and own my own company. I wouldn't ever have become a Director of a big company with over 1500 people. All of this made me a stronger person.

I would have probably ended up like little Sam and Harry the Horse; happy to stay in the factory till retirement, only to get made redundant before then.

Once you understand these principles, you open your eyes to the potentials and possibilities that you may never have understood or been aware of in the past – which I hadn't. Through education, I now do.

The Three Princes of Serendipity

The first of these principles is the Serendipity Principle, serendipity has been described as the capacity of making happy discoveries along the road of life, and I realise now I had made many happy discoveries.

The Serendipity Principle comes from the Persian fairy tale The Three Princes of Serendip; let me explain – these three princes travelled around the world coming upon experience after experience of misfortune and seeing disaster in the lives of others, but as a result their visits and happy discoveries made tragedy and disaster turn into great successes and happiness. This is what happened to me when I was lonely, no education, no money, no future and I was letting my family down. Now I realise that serendipity was coming to the fore all through my life.

The Old Farmer

The Three Princes of Serendip came across many disasters and situations as they travelled around the world, seeing all the unfortunate incidences that went on.

One of the occurrences concerned a farmer; his only son had thrown from the farmer's horse and had broken his leg, the horse had run off and was not to be found; the farmer was devastated, but the three princes told him not to worry – it's too soon to judge, and something good will happen. At the time the country was involved in a war with a neighbouring country, and the next morning a squad of soldiers arrived in the village to forcefully conscript the able-bodied men, and, as it happened, the farmer's only son had broken his leg so he was spared from conscription and from going to war. Later that day representatives from the government came to seize all of the horses so that the army could use them, but since the farmer's only horse had run off, again the farmer was spared. The army lost a great battle, and most of the men and the horses were killed; so, what appeared to be unfortunate events – the broken leg and the runaway horse turned out to be the farmer's salvation. Sometime after the war, the horse came home of its own accord leading several other wild horses to the farm, the son's leg was soon mended, and the farmer was happy, an apparent disaster had turned into a series of blessings in disguise.

Just as when I was mugged, riding my little bike; things happen for a reason. This sort of thing will happen to you as well, over and over, if you allow it to, and look for it.

I learned that the key to understanding serendipity is a principle of positive expectations, this principle says the more commonly you expect something to happen, the more likely it is to occur. I realise now that the Serendipity Principle was working for me all my life, and it has probably been working for you. Look back into your life and check it out.

Confidently Expect

The one common denominator of serendipitous events is that they only occur when you are completely confident that all things will work out for the best – and this is what people go through life without realising. Maybe they had no future, but confidently expected, year in and year out, that one day something good would happen; they were always looking for some good in every setback and difficulty, and that's what we've all got to do.

It doesn't matter how things are going, you've got to confidently expect that good things will occur – use the Principle of Serendipity and surprisingly all kinds of happy coincidences will take place; many of which initially appear to be failures or unfortunate events, will turn out to be happy and confident events. Which events now, do you feel in your life are a disaster or are hurting you? If you use the Law of Expectations with confidence, serendipitous events will happen in your life. So, come on, look back at your life right now, and you'll learn from every situation that you have been in, and you didn't realise that at the time that it was learning curve.

Part of my Education

I realise now that be being on the dole and getting mugged while riding my little bike, were part of my education. If you confidently expect, when things are going wrong for you, that there is going to be a happy event, and there is going to be a learning situation within it, that is when the Principle of Serendipity will start to work for you - happy events like in the story of the Three Princes. Encouraging people, saying that better things will happen. At that time in my life, my career and my business were not going well, things were not right, but looking back now, I realise that the situation was exactly what I needed.

Now don't forget, I left school when I was 14½. I worked in a factory for 18 years with no further education, but with the help of mentors, friends, family and dark nights of the soul I climbed up the ladder of success. That thick Liverpool lad became a regional director with a top company in charge of 1500 people, earning huge money.

You're in the Right Situation Right Now

Now regarding my education, here is an important psychological principle. I found out that the situation, at this moment, is exactly what you need for your own personal growth and development. Every part of your life is exactly as it should be, every difficulty you're facing or dealing with today contains within it possibilities that you can turn to your advantage, to achieve the kind of life that you want for yourself. That's what was happening to me. I was working in a challenging industry, things weren't going right for me, and I was there just to get some respite.

The Zone

There is a mental state, where you feel and perform at your very best – called being 'in the zone' – have you ever been in the zone? It's a common phrase in athletics; when you emotionalise your mind, clarify your thoughts, intensify your desires and approach your life with confident, positive expectations all sorts of serendipitous and synchronised events begin to appear in your life, as they did for me – John Haynes. It has also happened for many millions of other people. The only relationship that these events have with each other is the meaning that you give them, by the thoughts that you think. Alas, my thoughts in my early years were fuzzy, confused and contradictory, and these principles did not work for me at that time, or for many other people. This lack of clarity is the primary reason that most people are unhappy and unsuccessful like I was, they have potentially enormous powers, but they are failing to use them. The average person, as you know, has a hundred billion brain cells, we're unique, we're different, but we don't know how to use these powers, these laws to the best advantage because we don't understand how they work. So, let me explain.

Here's another example of synchronicity and this is a true story. I heard this many years ago, through educating my mind by reading books; remember my professor with Big Sally, he had said that I should read for half an hour in the morning and half an hour at night. That equates to one book per week. Four books per month, and if you keep the neural groove habit going, that's fifty books per year.

Synchronicity

So, like many top people, I studied synchronicity and serendipity, clarity and goal setting, and this true story made me think.

There was a person who was not happy with his job, going nowhere, and because he was unhappy with his job, he used to go home at night and moan at his children and his wife. One day, he and his wife talked about how much better he would feel if he could find a different job and earn more money, possibly in a different field. They discussed how they would like to do things better for their children, and he really wanted to change jobs. The next night they got invited out for a meal by some friends, to a nice restaurant, but the restaurant was fully booked, and they couldn't get a table. So, instead of heading home, they went to another restaurant nearby. When they sat down to eat, they realised that on the next table was a friend that they had not seen in years, the friend and his wife were with another couple – they started to talk to each other, catching up and reminiscing about the old days, and as they were talking he explained that he was tired, fed up with his job and was looking to move on and give his family a better standard of living. The man on the other table explained that there were opportunities in his industry, and that they might have jobs which would provide him with better prospects, he passed him his number and asked him to call. So, he called the next day and made an appointment.

Honesty is the Best Policy

This appointment appeared out of the blue, the man that had given him the number had understood that he was ready to move on, into a role with more prospects so that he could look after his family better and grow personally – the man was so impressed by his first impressions in the restaurant that he gave him a job. He had liked his honesty and integrity and realised that he wasn't in denial. Well, the man took the position that he was offered, and within a year had doubled his income and was earning far more than he had ever done throughout his life.

Most people would say, wow, he was in the right place at the right time, and that he was lucky, but you know by now that this is an example of synchronicity. The young man had been clear, confident and honest that he wanted a better life for him and his family, and as a result it triggered off a series of events created by the forces of the universe that not only cancelled one reservation, but opened another that put him precisely with the right person, at the right time at the right table! Would you believe it? The man, that night could have stayed at home, feeling down, feeling miserable and sat in front of the TV, and maybe had a few drinks – but no, he went out with his friends to a restaurant which was full, but decided then to go to another restaurant, which reunited him with an old friend, who was with another friend, and that other person gave him the opportunity to move on with his life.

People might say that he made his own luck by taking action, just as you need to do when you're down, and you're fed up, when nothing is going right – take action – his actions triggered synchronicity and serendipity! Now, I've told you all about that because I'm convinced, in my heart, that that's what happened to me in life.

Why did I go to work in Hygena? Was it a total mistake? Because it wasn't my music inside, but something inside of me, the still small voice from within. I just wanted a better life for myself, I wanted to improve, and because I found these workmates in the Hygena factory, synchronicity and serendipity were teaching me a lesson.

I will explain all that happened to me in the years to come because of the synchronised and serendipitous events in my life, from being in the right place at the right time. So, just keep believing; if it happened to John Haynes, it could happen to you.

When you're down when you're fed up, believe in your heart that some good will come out of it. Keep believing in confident expectations, keep saying to yourself, "I confidently expect that I'm going to have a better life, I confidently expect that I'll get rid of all my debts, I confidently expect that good things will happen to me." If you keep believing in that, synchronicity will come to the forefront. Serendipity will be there for you, and all the universe. So, keep believing.

'I flew with the eagles and The Three Princes of Serendipity.'

Accelerate your memory:
1. What is mental preparation?
2. Who did I meet when my billiard balls were bouncing into each other?
3. What does serendipity mean?
4. How do you implement confident expectations?
5. Why was being made redundant from the Hygena the big turning point of my life?
6. When you're down, but you keep taking action, what do you trigger?
7. What happened when the positive man bumped into an old friend in a restaurant?
8. What does synchronicity mean?
9. What does the small voice inside mean?
10. Explain the situation you are in right now; is it where you should be at this very moment in time?

'If the rate of change outside your organisation is greater than the rate of change inside your organisation, then the end is in sight.' Jack Welch of General Electric.

8. KENYA

The speaker boomed, "Papa John of England, please come to the platform."

My heart froze. My pulse increased. The sweat rolled down my face. My mind asked me inquisitively, "What am I doing here? Why have I put myself in this situation?"

Because there I was in Kenya; in the heart of Mombasa, in one of its most chaotic times in history, when tribal war had broken out all over the country and where Kenyan villagers were brutally killing each other. It was world news - plastered on every TV channel from here to Timbuktu! Most people in the world had been told by their government not to travel there as it was too dangerous. But there I was in between it all in the country's second largest city. Home to one and a half million people!

I shook uncontrollably as I walked up to the platform. Suddenly the world press appeared. And because I was one of the few white men at this rally, caught in this monumental city between warring tribes, the cameras rolled in on me.

They asked me if I wished to give a talk and my heart started to pound. My subconscious mind was drowning. How did I end up here of all places? Let me explain...

Fifteen years earlier, I'd travelled to Kenya with my partner Linda. It was a holiday I'd promised her for many years. One that I would present to her on a suitably special occasion in her life; somewhere magnificent. But you know what the typical man is like. We've got an unfortunate habit of promising things and then procrastinating. We always think there's enough time!

So, with a year to go until the big day, Linda suddenly approached me; "Where am I going on my special birthday?"

Having not done anything as of yet, I hastily replied; "It's a secret."

The interrogation wasn't over yet, however. Intrigued, she said, "Give me a clue."

I calmed her down by telling her not to worry and that she would be delighted with my choice. But as it often does, life gets in the way. We work hard, and we forget things. And so, I was just as surprised six months later when Linda cornered me again with the same question as half a year earlier.

I replied with a little white lie "Linda, stop getting impatient. Everything is arranged."

However, when it got to just three months to go, I told myself that it was time to start planning this special holiday for real and book it; a notion I didn't return to until two weeks before we were due to go. Linda unbeknown to me couldn't stop thinking about the holiday. She was already packed; her passport was ready, and I regrettably had done diddly squat.

I rushed down to the travel agency. My heart was in my mouth. Once again, I had shown the proud skills of procrastination! The thief of time.

I pleaded with the poor lady at the desk "I want to book an extraordinary holiday right now. Somewhere luxurious. Somewhere where not many people have ventured to. Somewhere where our breath will be taken away. Please, please help me!"

The kind looking lady could plainly see the stress in my face, the glare in my eyes and got to it straight away; "I will do it for you, Mr Haynes."

Sydney, Abu Dhabi, India. Each time I said no. It had to be somewhere special, different and completely unique. We went through about ten different countries and reaching the end of my tether; I got angry with myself. Why hadn't I booked it a year earlier?

Suddenly, a particular country sparked my interest. Kenya.

I said "Kenya? Is that where the lions, tigers and big elephants are?" Delighted we were getting somewhere, at last, the lady exclaimed, "Yes, Mr Haynes yes!"

Wow! I was over the moon and told her to make the reservation straightaway. She then asked me if I wanted to look at the hotels. However, much to her surprise, I told her that I trusted her, and just to let me know all the arrangements when she could. I left the travel agents in a rush. The next port of call was to get my passport sorted.

Two days later, the agency phoned me up with all of the arrangements. The holiday was paid for, the passports were renewed, and there we were ready for our holiday of a lifetime.

Leaving behind a rainy Manchester Airport, I turned to Linda; "You wanted a holiday that's different and unique. That's what Kenya is all about! You will love it."

She congratulated me on my surprising choice but then asked the question I feared the most, "What's the hotel like? Is it a five star? A seven?"

No clue as to what our accommodation was like, I replied: "Wait until you see it, Linda.'"

After the trauma of the last few weeks, I was just relieved we were safe and sound on the plane!

We got there and unloaded our suitcases. A big coach with a load of tourists en route to all the luxurious hotels along the golden Kenyan coast was waiting for us.

An hour of smooth travelling passed, and we witnessed many excited people get off and waving goodbye to us as they stepped into their incredible resorts. Linda was excited, at each drop-off, wishing she was following their footsteps.

After an hour and a half, it was just us on the coach. I calmed Linda's curiosities, "It must be a fantastic hotel," but then another hour went by, and the roads started to change. No more gliding along. We were now getting caught in pothole after pothole. There were no traffic signs — nothing at all that resembled city life.

Incredibly another three hours passed, and we were still on the coach! This really had to be a special place. Unusual didn't seem to cover the half of it. The coach driver looked around at us, shaking his head in a disbelieving way; as if saying, if only you knew what you'd let yourself in for.

Linda was understandably frantic at this point. 'Where are

we going?'. I didn't dare answer.

We looked out of the window and saw among the barren, buildingless countryside a series of straw huts. Surely not - my stomach started to churn and not just because of all the nasty bumps we were encountering along the way.

Half an hour later, a small clearing along the edge of the Indian Ocean appeared out of nowhere, and a hotel seemed to rise out of the ashes.

Relieved, I turned to Linda, "I told you it would be unique."

The gates opened, the guards signalled us in, and we entered with trepidation. Unloading the luggage from the coach, one thing that hit us straight away was that there were not a lot of people in the hotel. The other thing that surprised us was how quickly the driver bolted. A weary smile, a disbelieving shake of the head and whoosh he was gone!

We were not left standing alone for long, though. Upon hearing of our arrival, the Hotel Manager had rushed down from his office and had given us an extremely eager welcome. For some reason, it seemed like he was not very used to meeting and greeting tourists! He sat us down, gave us some juice and told us about his beautiful hotel with swimming pools and so forth — the perfect place to relax, unwind and enjoy yourselves for two glorious weeks.

I looked at Linda thinking, "So far so good," but she was still coming to terms with the mammoth journey, the daunting prospect of staying in a straw hut and now the lack of tourists in the hotel. There's no pleasing some people.

The manager then lowered his voice 'Listen. What I'd advise you to do is to just stay in the hotel. We have all the facilities you need here. Believe me. Don't step outside the hotel!'

Stunned, we enquired why?, To which he responded that this place was unique (I turned to Linda in an I told you so glance) because it's in the heart of a real African village and the reason why not many tourists come to the hotel. Linda and I looked at each other. This really was something, unlike the norm! The manager then explained that the villagers, despite their good nature, aren't used to tourists and again advised us to stay put for the fortnight. We nodded our heads, crossed our hearts in mutual agreement and proceeded to settle in.

But it wasn't long before I started to develop itchy feet and being a typical inquisitive Brit; I was overly curious to see what the surrounding areas were like.

The next morning, I made my adventurous escape out of the hotel grounds and started walking along the beach to the jungle itself. Although from time to time, the Hotel Managers voice popped into my head with warnings of 'Don't leave the hotel grounds. The villagers aren't used to tourists!' I ignored these reminders and instead carried on wading further through the array of mesmerising trees as if in a fixed trance. Who knew what I would see on my travels? Lions and tigers and elephants. Oh my!

After about ten minutes, I couldn't see the way back to the beach and started to scramble. But when an hour flew by, and I was still in the same mess as before, it eventually dawned on me that I was lost deep in a Kenyan jungle! I became disorientated and started to follow any direction I could. Another half an hour passed by and increasingly covered in sweat; I was panicked by the realisation that I had no mobile phone on my person. I had no way to contact the outside world!

There seemed to be no light at the end of the tunnel, and I started to fear for my life.

With the thought of the elephants, the tigers and the ants disposing of my body etched on my brain; I then stumbled with amazement as much as sheer terror into the heart of a real Kenyan village. The children were routinely enjoying their breakfast over a lit campfire, but this tradition was shattered when they saw me, a giant white man, disturb their morning routine. They screamed. They couldn't believe it! The rest of the villagers; the mums, the dads, the grandparents looked at me in complete horror. Everybody froze for what seemed like a lifetime! Just enough time for me to gather my thoughts and remember something else that the Hotel Manager had said the night before. 'Jambo'. The Swahili word for 'Hello' and something he advised us that we should say if we were to encounter a villager.

I chanced my luck. "Jambo."

Nothing. Not even a flicker.

I repeated it twice. "Jambo, Jambo."

Suddenly, as if out of nothing, the elders in the village responded "Jambo."

Just then, a big grin appeared on their faces, and everybody all around me cheered and started to join in. I had been accepted! I beamed broadly and remembered that a smile always lifts another person's mood, increases self-esteem and lights up the brain like a dimmer switch. So, with this in mind, I continued to beam from ear to ear with Jambos aplenty!

It took about an hour, but it was one of the most beautiful experiences of my life when we started to communicate in something more than just the occasional Jambo. Having once been a British colony, the villagers had a broken grasp of the English language and started talking to me. They even offered me some watery soup! My heart felt safe. What a time to be alive!

After food, they even offered to walk me back to the hotel. A journey that took us more than two hours. But I didn't care. This was the start of my introduction to Kenya. A country I have now known inside out for twenty-three years and what led me eventually doing a talk in Mombasa.

The Villagers

When I got back to the hotel, the Hotel Manager knew that I had been outside of the grounds and approached me with one of those 'I told you so' talks. I interrupted him with the fact that I was British – a country known for its risk-takers and for never listening to anybody. He stormed off, and I went to find Linda and recall my amazing adventures with the beautiful, friendly and heart-warming Kenyan villagers.

Despite enjoying the hotel and all its facilities over the next couple of days, I soon got itchy feet again and thought of my morning in the jungle with the villagers. Having, finally, encouraged Linda to walk just half a mile from the hotel, we were soon met with the sight of a crowd of Kenyan villagers eagerly looking from behind the palm trees. We started to wave and could make out the big smiles appear on their faces. An uplifting feeling quite like no other!

Two mornings later, I found myself again walking along the golden beach and this time saw a hundred-strong crowd of children walking into the jungle and singing joyously as if they didn't have a care in the world. Intrigued, I waited until they were out of sight but the nagging thought of what they were doing bugged me for the rest of the day, so the next morning at the exact same time, I came down to the beach, saw the group once more in similarly high spirits and started to follow them. Curiosity had finally got the better of me!

After half an hour ducking and diving under branches, I was exhausted. With no transport in which to get from A to B in the village, the children were accustomed to walking very quickly, and it took me all my time to keep up with them. However, I stuck with it for a further three and a half miles before finally seeing the reason why the children were so enthusiastic. We had come to a clearance with a school in it.

Far from being a proper brick school with big burly gates like we know in the UK, this school was just a few huts with a small primitive fence around it. I thought it was brilliant. Three and a half hours walking on their own two feet, singing and yearning to come here. It must be a good school! As they approached the entrance, however, they all suddenly sat down, the singing subsided, and everything went quiet.

I found this all very confusing, so I approached them, "Come on, boys and girls, it's school time. Let's go in!"

One of the children stood up from the crowd of children aged between six and twelve and replied, "No school for us. We can't go to school. We are not allowed."

I was perplexed. Why couldn't they go to school? Surely everyone has the right to an education.

Suddenly, I saw a teacher out of the corner of my eye and approached him. He was startled that an Englishman was outside the school gates and introduced himself as Joseph, the Headmaster. What I later found out from him was that many of the villagers were called George, James and Bill, all christened with English names! After all, Kenya was in the recent past, a British colony.

It was about this time that I was given a name that would stick with me for the rest of my life; Papa John. The children called me this as to them; I was one of the oldest people they had ever met and this nickname; a cherished term of endearment stuck and went as far as the older villagers, the teachers and even those organising the talk twenty-three years later in Mombasa.

Back outside the school gates, I shook Joseph's hand and immediately launched into a tirade of questions of why they weren't allowed to come to school. How can this be so when in the UK, we will do anything to stay out of school yet here we have hundreds of kids walking such a long way, singing, dancing and wanting to get an education?

Joseph sympathised with me and the kids, "We can't take them because of money. For every teacher, there are a hundred children. It's impossible, and we don't have the books, the staff, the equipment. The government don't pay, so we have to ask the parents to pay, and a lot of them have no money." I was enraged and asked how long they had been denied the chance to go to school. Even though I half expected it, I was still stunned to hear Joseph's answer. Most of these children had never been to school.

I looked at the children and their smiling faces, that I had encountered from the crack of dawn this morning, had suddenly turned to sadness and despair. All they wanted was an education. I have always believed that the future belongs to the learner, and these poor children were being denied a future with no schooling. These children would wait outside the school all day, they would not only wait for their more fortunate friends to finish but wait in the hope that one of the teachers would be kind enough and let them in. Unfortunately, was never the case.

So, it was with a large tinge of regret that I waved goodbye to Joseph and the large crowd of children and returned down-hearted to the unnecessary luxuries of my hotel.

That evening whilst eating dinner with Linda, I was still upset and angry at about what I had found out that very same morning. Some children in Europe and the UK moan and whine about going to school, and yet it's free education! Surely there must be a way to get these Kenyan children to go to school.

Seeking inspiration, the following two mornings, I once again followed the children into the jungle this time joining in the singing and dancing and seeing their happy smiling faces hoping they would miraculously be allowed into school, all the while still racking my brains of what I could do to help. On the fourth morning, the lightbulb moment finally happened!

Have you ever met somebody, looked back years later and realised that if you hadn't met this person, your life would be completely different? Synchronicity and serendipity. He came into my life like a whirlwind. His name was Grasshopper. Let me tell you about my first encounter with this quite remarkable boy.

Grasshopper was one of these many unfortunate children that sat outside the school gates all day waiting for his friends to come out and play with him. He was seven at the time but had been trying to go to school since he was five. All he ever wanted was an education.

Now one of Joseph's roles as headmaster was to stop children trying to get into the school. And normally he was very adept at doing it, but this particular day, a bright sunny morning, some-body was distracting his attention at the school gates. Guess who? That's right.

With me being quite a talker, Grasshopper sensed that this was his big opportunity. So, while I was talking to Joseph, Grass-hopper made a bolt for it. Luckily, Joseph had his back to him, but I could see Grasshopper out of the corner of my eye running and building up speed, determined to get through the school gates.

Although Joseph turned around and spotted him, nothing was going to stop Grasshopper!

He shuffled, swerved and ran into the primitive classroom huts, with 100 children inside; Joseph's calls of, "No Grasshopper, you're not allowed into school," firmly in the distance.

Joseph ended our conversation there and then; "I'm sorry, Papa John, but I can't let Grasshopper into the school," and run after him. Not wanting to miss out on an eventful morning, I duly followed.

Sometimes you find yourself in a situation where you can't believe what you're seeing. This was certainly one of those moments — a hundred children sitting on a barren floor. No seats. No desks. Just a hundred youngsters looking up at me in amazement thinking, "Who's this big white man with blonde-grey hair?"

All of them with big smiles on their faces, gleaming eyes focused in my direction. It was incredible! As we looked around the crowd, there was Grasshopper.

Do you remember when you were a child, and you closed your eyes and used to think that if you can't see them, then they can't see you? Well, Grasshopper was acting this out to a tee. He had his head down between his knees, thinking this of Joseph. But with every other boy and girl grinning from ear to ear, teeth gleaming brightly, Grasshopper really did stick out like a sore thumb.

Joseph went over to him wearily, as if he'd done it many times before, "Come on Grasshopper. I'm so sorry but no school today."

Grasshopper, distraught at being caught, looked up at us slowly with tears welling up in his eyes. His fight to go to school had been denied once more. Surrendering, Joseph gently took his hand and escorted him out of the school gates leaving all of his other 100 friends shouting after him. They all felt so sad for their friend. My heart was breaking. Surely there was a way to let him into school. I said exactly this to Joseph.

He looked at me; "No, Papa John. We don't have the money. Grasshopper will need books, and we just don't have the funds."

With this in mind, the right side of my brain flickered into action, and I proposed an idea. "Joseph, couldn't I pay for his education?"

Joseph was stunned, "It's a lot of money."

I told Joseph I didn't care. I wanted to help in some form, and this could be the best way to do it. I looked down at Grasshopper whilst saying this, and he looked up at me in amazement with a big smile on his face. If looks could melt hearts!

I asked Joseph how much it was to pay for Grasshopper to go to school for the whole year. All sorts of numbers went around my brain. For Grasshopper though, it was like Christmas Day or winning the lottery. He was jumping up and down with excitement screaming my name; "Papa John. Papa John."

"Five hundred pounds," Joseph replied. That seemed reasonable to me.

"That's a year's education, a satchel, two school uniforms and a pair of shoes to walk around in because of all the sharp pebbles and stone, he said.

I weighed up the pros and cons, but my mind was already made up. Five hundred pounds for a youngster's future, a youngster's schooling; to give them a better life, a better future. The only way they're going to grow and have a good life with family is through education and so all things discussed, it was an absolute bargain! What're five hundred pounds in the UK? We go drinking. We dine out extravagantly at restaurants. We buy unnecessary clothes and gadgets.

"I will pay for it, Joseph. Please let me sponsor Grasshopper!"

Joseph was elated and started shaking my hand, "Papa John, that's so generous!"

All of the children were jumping up and down and hugging each other, even though they weren't being sponsored. They were just so happy that Papa John was going to give Grasshopper a chance of an education, at the age of seven, for the very first time! Like Grasshopper, I felt on top of the world.

Joseph assured me that he would get everything ready; the school uniform, the books organised as well as letting his parents know. I promised that I would be there at half-past seven the very next day and, buoyantly, I went back to the hotel to tell Linda the good news. The sounds of children's cheers ringing in my ears!

When I got back, the hotel manager was there waiting for me. I couldn't help but tell him what had happened in the jungle and much to my surprise, he was pleased with what I had to say and applauded my generosity.

Linda was just as excited as me when I told her and later that night, we both reflected on the day's events.

It's strange sometimes when you book a holiday, and you want to go to relax in the sun or next to the pool, and it works out differently; but like Einstein famously said, 'The purpose of life is to make a difference in another person's life.' That couldn't be anywhere nearer the truth. I had the warmest of glows inside of me.

I couldn't wait for the morning to come, and when it did, I rushed to the school gates early with excitement. Never mind Grasshopper, this was like my first day at school! I found myself trembling with anticipation. I didn't have to wait too long.

Joseph and two parents were followed by a young boy looking as pleased as punch.

He was dressed in little shorts, a little school uniform, a satchel with books in it and was being cheered on by a group of excited schoolchildren. It could only be Grasshopper.

He looked up at me with the biggest smile on his face and with a, "Thank you, Papa John," he proudly walked through the school gates.

A big cheer rose up in the crowd, and everybody started clapping this quite remarkable seven-year-old boy. There were no tinges of jealousy from the others who weren't allowed in—just pure adulation for their friend.

I felt like a million dollars when I passed Joseph over the

check for five hundred pounds.

Suddenly, Joseph handed me the check back. "No, no, Papa John. It's the wrong amount."

I knew it was too good to be true. It was clear Joseph meant to say five thousand pounds. I shrugged it off. The glow of satisfaction on Grasshopper's face was worth its weight in gold on its own! It's like when you give money to a worthy cause. It just feels so good. It puts you standing on the side of angels.

'Not five hundred pounds. Too many zeroes. Fifty pounds.'

I was stunned. I was shocked to my core. Fifty pounds for a full year's education. Uniform, books, everything. I spend double that on a meal in a restaurant. This really was another world to back home! Just then, it hit me like a bolt of lightning.

I turned to Joseph, "I've committed to paying five hundred pounds now. Keep it. It's all yours - wait. Does that mean I could sponsor another nine children?"

Joseph looked at me. He couldn't believe what I was saying. Was this a wind-up? Seeing that it wasn't, he hugged me. I had the answer I was searching for.

When Joseph told the children, it was as if Kenya had won the World Cup! The biggest roar. The loudest cheers. A stampede of feet jumping up and down on the floor. Nine of them were going to be given a chance to go to school, just like their friend Grasshopper. Seeing all their happy faces looking up at me, I couldn't choose, so I chickened out and asked Joseph to select the lucky few. I hadn't got the heart to turn any of them down.

Twenty-four hours later, there I was again. Same place. Same time. The same warm feeling inside. Just this time, I had Linda there with me; holding my hand tightly, proud at what I'd done to help this amazing village. And there they appeared around the corner, nine children in little school shoes, a brand-new uniform and satchels, all going to school with Grasshopper. Just like before, there was no envy and spite from the other children waiting outside the gates. Instead, the sounds of singing that took me back to that very first day, I encountered them along the beach.

This was the start of me helping this beautiful Kenyan village. The start of an epic journey that helped shape the whole of my life and what gave me my destiny forever.

9. ACRES OF DIAMONDS

When you're a child, you're programmed from infancy to believe that someone or something else is responsible for much of your life. When you are a child you are fortunate that your parents take care of everything you do, they provide you with food, shelter, clothing, education, opportunities, recreation, money, medical attention; it's great when you're a child, you are a passive player in the process.

Then the problems begin when you become an adult, with unconscious expectations that somewhere, somehow, someone is still responsible for you. See we grew up, in all fairness, in the habit of not having responsibility. We get taken to school, pocket money, we get educated, we get fed and the neural groove in the mind, just goes on with this – don't forget it take 21 days for the mind to get into new habits, so, let's face it, it takes years and years as we are in a deep rut!

We are in a comfort zone and not taking any responsibility for our lives, and then when we get into the working environment, we expect the that it's a habit of the boss to take responsibility for giving us money every week/month. We still expect the government to do its bit; we still expect the NHS to look after our bodies, why should we take responsibility? We've never taken responsibility before, and that is one of the biggest failures in life, we don't take responsibility for anything and, in all fairness, it becomes a habit. But the time comes when we have to take responsibility. When you're grown up, at the age of 18, your subconscious mind is ready, but there was Grasshopper taking responsibility for the whole of his being at the age of 14. How many people do you know in their 50s and 60s that still don't take responsibility for their lives, blaming and getting angry with everyone else, it's like being stuck in a revolving door, and asking someone else to push it as it's not their responsibility! Can you see it? That's where society has gone wrong.

So can you see that the problems begin when people come into our adult life with unconscious expectations, you've got to take responsibility but realise that from the age of 18 onwards (sometimes earlier), you are in the driving seat (like Grasshopper) and that you are the architect of your own destiny. Whether or not your parents have succeeded in raising you to be a totally self-reliant individual, with high self-esteem and high self-confidence, and brought you up the right way; from the age of 18, you should be responsible. They say once you take responsibility, that's the time when you really start to grow up and have a wonderful life – just like Grasshopper.

You see, the acceptance of complete responsibility, giving up all your excuses is not easy. I find that it's one of the hardest things that you could ever attempt, that's why most people never do it, it's like putting on a parachute and jumping out of a plane for the first time. It's both scary and exhilarating when you cast free, you suddenly feel completely alone and completely vulnerable, however, in a few moments you start to feel a rush of excitement, your heart starts to pound fast, and you feel remarkably happy and free. You can never give responsibility away; the only thing that you can do is give away control. The Law of Control, you can only feel good about yourself based on the degree that you are in control of your own life. If you try to make someone else responsible for your life, you end up giving them control over your emotions and your peace of mind; this dawned on me as Grasshopper was talking.

I realised that those children from those villages in Kenya never moaned or complained even at the age of 6 or 7. I used to watch them wading into the sea, or looking for berries climbing up the palm trees to get coconuts, and stupidly I used to ask, "What are you doing all this for?" And they would look at me and say with big smiles on their faces, "Papa John, if we don't catch the fish, or get the coconuts from the tree then we go very hungry Papa John." They were taking responsibility for feeding their own bellies at the age of 6 or 7. I would watch them take roots from trees polishing their teeth, and I would ask what they were doing with those 'dirty' roots. They would explain that if they didn't clean their teeth with the roots, then they would get a very bad toothache, they were taking responsibility for making sure their teeth were always clean, as there was no dentist. If they got a toothache, the only way to fix it was to remove the tooth. They took responsibility for everything they did. They were never envious or angry; they would never blame anyone else; they were happy inside as they were taking responsibility for everything in their lives. If it's to be, it's up to me. Wow, and there was Grasshopper taking full responsibility for everything, for his brothers, his sisters, and his education. It's a massive learning curve. I know that I can be one of the losers in life, I moan, and I whine, and it's everyone else's fault – the government, the doctor, the boss, my parent's fault as they brought me into the world, I was now getting educated by these beautiful villagers – especially Grasshopper.

John Paul Getty said, *'The man who comes up with a means for doing or producing almost anything better, faster or more economically has his future and his fortune at his fingertips.'*

This made me think about Grasshopper; he wanted to take responsibility for his family, his future, and everything else. As he was looking at me with his bright gleaming eyes, expecting to get on a plane with me and come to Liverpool, my mind was going back many years, and I remember reading an article about the ability you have right now to achieve anything you want to. I was feeling this about Grasshopper – he had the ability to achieve far more than he had. He had the ability and determination, and because he had the ability to learn any skills needed to do any job that he wanted to do, he could achieve any goal that he could set for himself. I was thinking all this and realising that there was no way to get him back to Liverpool, I was embarrassed, I didn't want to break his heart and tell him it was impossible, so I looked at him again and then it came to me.

As you know, we have a left-brain hemisphere and a right-brain hemisphere. The left is the analytical side, the facts and the figures, and the left-brain takes all the information in and makes decisions on that information. It's said that the left of the brain only has a short-term memory, and sometimes this is why schools and universities fall down. They give out all the information, and the left-brain takes it all in, but if all this knowledge and learning is not processed by the right side of the brain that deals with long-term memory, emotions, arts, and creativity, up to 70% of this knowledge can be forgotten. Lucky enough, I've been doing accelerated learning for many years, using mind maps and visualisation; learning how to relax and transfer that knowledge to the right-brain. I was wondering how I would get out the delicate situation, of telling Grasshopper how he could not achieve the dream of coming to Liverpool to earn money for his family.

It is said that 'Your subconscious mind is an enormous memory bank that has been storing and sorting EVERYTHING that has ever happened to you. By the time you reach the age of 21, the amount of data received and stored is 100 x the contents of the Encyclopaedia Britannica—that's 32 volumes—32,640 pages of 40 million on half a million topics!' But we just don't know how to retrieve that knowledge.

Because I'd been learning about the nine stages of accelerated learning, suddenly, a story came back to me, just as I was about to tell Grasshopper the bad news. I said, 'Grasshopper, hold on, can I tell you a story?' And he grinned at me because he knew that stories and knowledge were powerful, and these beautiful Kenyan villagers and children love stories. He said 'Yes, Papa John' and so I asked him to sit down. There I was, at 6 o'clock in the morning, thousands of miles from home, telling Grasshopper the story of 'Acres of Diamonds' by Russell Conwell (1843 – 1925).

This story has been told around the world many times over, and it was told to me when I was going through a difficult time, when I was a Company Director on the verge of leaving my job and moving on. "So," I said to Grasshopper, "This story 'Acres of Diamonds' was based on a parable Conwell heard while travelling through present-day Iraq in 1870, and this is the version that was told to me."

"OK, Grasshopper. Once there was a farmer that ploughed his fields, though he hated his job, but was always moaning and grumpy, he farmed under the burning sun and used to whip his horse to get it to move faster. He was always cursing and shaking his fist at the sky asking God why he had been condemned to such awful work, he was trying to plant seeds to grow corn to sell, but he never had any success. He was so miserable that when the neighbouring farmers asked for his help in rebuilding a barn that had burnt down, he said to them, 'Get off my land, I have enough to do without taking on another person's worries and problems.' They walked away, angry and bewildered by his nasty comments."

"The farmer had two sons and a lovely wife, but because he was always angry, he blamed everyone else for his predicament, so when he went home at night he took his frustrations out on his family, screaming at the sons to be quiet, and moaning if his tea wasn't ready."

I looked at Grasshopper and continued, "So, Grasshopper, one day a traveller passed by, the traveller had been travelling for four weeks and hadn't seen a soul on his journey, he was thirsty, hungry and in need of food, water and a place to wash. The farmer was not happy; he growled, 'what do you think this is? An Inn. I'm a farmer; I have enough on my plate. I've got demanding neighbours, a wife and two sons that never cooperate, and who are always shouting and screaming and are never happy, and now you! No sir, I can't help, get off my land.' The traveller was stunned he couldn't believe that the first person he had seen in four weeks was so angry and bitter. He got on his horse and said, "damn you, sir, I'll find my own fortune; at least where I'm going, hundreds of miles away, it might be dirty and scruffy, like you, but it's covered in acres of diamonds. Goodbye, sir.' This made the farmer think; his land was also scruffy and dirty, hmmm!"

Once an idea is planted in the subconscious mind, it's like an acorn; it begins to mature and grows like an old oak tree. "So, Grasshopper, the farmer woke up one morning and told himself that he no longer wanted to work the land; under the burning sun, with horrible neighbours and a wife and sons that didn't love him, so he screams at his wife, 'It's over, the marriage is finished.' 'No,' she cries, 'I love you; I love you.' 'It's over,' he said, 'I'm going to sell the farm, and go to a far-off land and find my acres of diamonds.'"

I looked at Grasshopper and explained to him that in those times, life was very hard and very cruel, but he didn't understand how someone would do that to their family. So, I continued, "The farmer sold the land for a pittance, and he said goodbye to his family, who now had to fend for themselves, and he went in search of his own acres of diamonds." Grasshopper was nearly in tears, "Papa John" he said, "that's so cruel, his poor wife and sons."

I carried on with the story, "After nearly six weeks he found the grubby land, and he believed that underneath it would be acres and acres of diamonds. So, he got off his horse and starts kicking at the ground; then he realises that he'll have to buy a pickaxe, and a shovel and a tent to sleep in, and thinks maybe if I work a bit harder tomorrow, I'll find something! He spent his leftover money on what he needed and spent the next days and weeks digging for his acres of diamonds, trying different parts of the land, shovelling, cursing, and still angry. But he didn't find the acres of diamonds. After two months, when all the other prospectors left upon realising that there were no acres of diamonds in the land, he still wouldn't give up. He kept going on. One day while he was working, a rattlesnake startled his horse, which ran away never to be seen again. He had no money, he was running out of supplies, but he persevered until he was the last prospector mining for acres of diamonds. The farmer began to reflect on how his life had been; he realised what he had done; he had no money or supplies. He realised his mistake in giving up his boys, his own flesh and blood and his lovely wife, he realised that she had loved him, she had put up with his moaning and whining, for so long, and he knew he had done the wrong thing. He had made the biggest mistake of his life; he had left his home and family for a dream that was impossible to achieve."

By this time Grasshopper's eyes were popping out of his head. "The farmer climbed up to the highest cliff and left a note, apologising for all his mistakes, saying how much he loved his family, and that there were no acres of diamonds. As he was about to jump, he suddenly thought about his old neighbours, and wondered how come they had grown corn; they had the same sun, the same land, how was it that their families were happy. He was feeling very sorry for himself; there was no such thing as acres of diamonds. He jumped into the river from the highest cliff and drowned." Grasshopper was distraught, "But Papa John, it's a mortal sin to take your own life, it's so sad, Papa John."

"I know Grasshopper," I said. "But meanwhile, Grasshopper, back on the old farm, the new owner had taken control, he had three little daughters and a wife. He had the same burning sun, and a horse to pull the plough, and he worked and worked on the land."

"You see Grasshopper, sometimes a glass can be seen as half empty or half full, and this farmer was optimistic, he had confident expectations, he knew that if he planted the seeds that the corn would grow. He was more than willing to join the other farmers to help paint a neighbour's house. Now, Grasshopper" I said, "They call this sowing and reaping. If you help another person, they will help you."

Even the famous Zig Ziglar once said, 'Give, give, give again.'

"The new farmer was more than willing to help the neighbours, he didn't have much, but he loved his wife, and spent time with his daughters; and because they were happy inside, they were happy on the outside. It was a hard, cruel life, but they were together as a family, and that's what matters."

Grasshopper smiled. "One day three strangers arrived, they

said, like the visitor to the original farmer, 'Farmer you are the first person we've seen in weeks, farmer, could we please have some water, some food, somewhere to wash up, please can you help us?' He said 'Certainly, gentlemen, I'd be delighted to help you! Come back to my farmhouse, we don't have too much, but I'm sure my wife can manage some coffee and biscuits.'"

"Well, Grasshopper, the three strangers were diamond merchants going to the big city, they came to the house and spoke to his lovely wife and asked the children about school. The farmer was happy inside from helping other people. Suddenly, one of the diamond merchants said to the farmer, 'Farmer, if you don't mind me asking, what are all these dirty rocks on your windowsill and mantlepiece, why have rocks in the house?' And the farmer beamed at the strangers and said, 'Well gentlemen, we might not have much paraffin to light the lamps at night, but when the moon shines through our window the rocks sparkle, and it lightens the whole of the room. Sometimes even enough for the girls to read by their light,' The stranger looked at him strangely and checked out the barren landscape through the window. He picked up one of the dirty rocks and blew on it. He cleaned it, rubbed at it, cleaned it a little more, and suddenly he could see the sparkles, he got out his jewellers' eyeglass and looked at it for a bit longer, he looked so shocked. Suddenly, he started to jump up and down and said, 'Quick, look at this, please,' so the visitors all got their eyeglasses out, inspected the rock and started jumping up and down. 'Farmer,' they said, 'this is not a dirty old rock, this is a diamond, the biggest we've ever seen.' So, they began to inspect all the other rocks exclaiming at each of them, 'These are the biggest diamonds we have ever seen.' Everyone was hugging each other with delight; when they asked where the farmer had found the rocks, he explained that they were off his dirty land and just popped up whenever he kicked the soil! The diamond merchants looked at each other and said to the farmer, 'Farmer, out there on your land; you have acres and acres of diamonds.'"

Grasshopper looked at me "Papa John, but the old farmer left his family, went hundreds of miles away to find acres of diamonds and all the time they were under his feet."

"Exactly Grasshopper. They do say that when God made us all, he broke the mold. We've all got this special talent and special skill, and if we find it, that's our acres of diamonds. The old farmer because he was grumpy, and he was a quitter, left his own land to find better fortune elsewhere. However, it was under his own feet. He had his acres of diamonds, and some people I know leave Liverpool to go to other cities, as they can't find work, or they leave the UK to emigrate hoping for a better life. But all the time, Grasshopper, under our own feet are acres of diamonds. We can make ourselves happy; we have to find a job that we love, we have to find that music, that's what life is about, all the time we have acres and acres of diamonds in our soul, in our heart, our abilities and our skills."

I added, "Grasshopper, find your music inside from within, and that's your acre of diamonds." He looked at me, and there he was age 14 with a clever mind, he was in shock. He said, "Papa John, Grasshopper goes now, Grasshopper needs to think," and he walked away with his head down; I watched him walk for about half a mile. I was relieved, at least I didn't have to tell him that it was an impossible dream, and I'd given him food for thought.

The next day I was out finding the water wells, building the straw huts, coaching the children on the beach, and no Grasshopper, the same the following day.

On the third day, I saw Grasshopper waiting for me, "Papa John, Papa John," he cried. When I asked how he was, he said, "Papa John, please don't cry, I have some sad news for you, Grasshopper decide not to leave village, Grasshopper needs to find his own acre of diamonds here. Grasshopper is not coming to Liverpool with you; please don't cry." Of course, I was so pleased that I didn't have to break his heart by telling him it was impossible to go to Liverpool. I said, "Grasshopper, I am so disappointed, I booked the plane, sorted everything out for you." '

I'm sorry Papa John' he said, "I need to stay here and find my own music inside and my own acres of diamonds."

"It's a wise move," I told him, "I respect your decision."

With that, he left, and my wife and I flew back to Liverpool. That story, I assure you changed my life. I was on the verge of leaving a Directorship in a big company; I was getting tired. I was the grumpy old farmer; nothing was going right. I didn't like my bosses and my clients moaning, and I got so fed up, that when eventually another company approached me and offered me acres of diamonds, more money, a better location and I was on the verge of quitting my job. The boss I worked for didn't like me, and the feeling was mutual. I was just about to hand in my notice, I had told my secretary, confidentially, what I was going to do. As I was thanking her for her support, another of the secretaries, a strong-willed lady called Joyce said, "John Haynes, I'm ashamed of you, you tell the 'acres of diamonds' story to everyone, and here you are like the old farmer quitting and going to another company. How dare you go back on your word, you should stay and find YOUR acres of diamonds, work a bit harder, get new skills, and one day with confident expectations something good will happen to you." She shocked me that much; she was so stern, I hesitated, thought about it, and then tore up my letter of resignation, and because I stayed, I improved my skills.

Exactly nine months later, the boss who was making my life hell got the sack, and because I'd been working on my skills and knowledge, they promoted me into his position. Joyce said to me, "I told you, John Haynes, that if you stayed, you would find your own acres of diamonds."

Anyway, the next year we went back to Kenya.

Grasshopper

So, when I had returned to the UK, my mind was on Grasshopper. Would he find his acres of diamonds? Would he find his music inside? All he wanted to do was build a straw roof for his beautiful parents, earn enough money for his education, and find his soulmate. I was wondering how he was getting on. But there he was, he didn't have a penny to his name, and he was practically starving to death like the other villagers who were short of food, and short of water.

In my studies, in my lifetime, I came to a certain point where I changed my attitude towards myself, and it changed the rest of my career. I realised that everyone that was at the top in any field had once been at the bottom like me! Anyone who is at the front of the line today was once at the back. Everyone at the top of the ladder of success had once been at the bottom and climbed up a rung at a time. This made me think of Grasshopper; he could climb up the ladder of success. Maybe he is at the back of the queue now, but this young man with his confidence, determination and his confident expectations, he could go to the top. The truth is that you are just as good in your area as anyone else you might ever meet. I thought about Grasshopper, if he decided to be the best in his chosen field, the only person that could stop him in his success is himself. The limits of excellent performance are the inner attitude of your mind, not the outer aspects of your life, and I know Grasshopper has a great inner life! He has values; he has honesty. Remember, it doesn't matter where you have come from, it only matters where you are going, and your future is only limited by your imagination and Grasshopper had a great imagination. He can learn anything he needs to learn to achieve any goal he can set for himself; he can excel at anything that he really loves and does. He was willing to make the necessary effort – and this applies to us all! Any goal attracts problems and to have something new we need to learn something new; Grasshopper would go into this with determination.

So, that year quickly passed, and I was really looking forward to going back with Linda to this beautiful village. After all, their love, their smiles, their attitude, the way they took responsibility, they had educated me. But the main thought on my mind as I flew from Manchester to Mombasa was that I hoped that Grasshopper had found his acres of diamonds, that one skill, that God's gift. We got to the village after a long journey, and straight away lots of villagers were around us, in the days that followed we started coaching the children, helping the ladies find water wells, look for straw roofs to fix, and of course, of course, what was going through my mind, and what I kept asking was, "Where is Grasshopper, has he found his acres of diamonds?" The villagers told me that they hadn't seen Grasshopper for a long time, and that concerned me, but we were so busy in the village teaching and talking, we went into the schools, and took the local teachers to the local hotel (they had never been in a hotel before). The kind owner let us give them lectures there, and we taught them how to teach using the nine stages of accelerated learning. See, the nine stages use whole brain learning; you can teach, motivate and inspire and channel the knowledge into the right-brain, which will last forever. They say the biggest mismatch in teaching is the mismatch between the teachers' teaching style and the pupils' learning style, the pupil will not learn correctly and the knowledge will not go into the long-term memory, and we taught these teachers the nine stages, and they excelled at the highest level. Children now are being taught the correct way.

Where was Grasshopper? Sadly, our three weeks went very quickly, we enjoyed the company of the villagers, but where was Grasshopper?

The next year arrived very quickly; we took off from Manchester with hope in our hearts that we would find Grasshopper and that he would have found his acres of diamonds. But when we got there, once again, there was no Grasshopper. Linda and I were concerned, she thought maybe I shouldn't have told him the acres of diamonds story, we asked, but nobody had seen him for a long time. I realised there and then that in this village if children go missing, they go missing, and that was the end of it! In other parts of the world, if a child goes missing, there are search parties and helicopters, but there was no such thing here. I remember that during my first visit, I was encouraging the children to write down their own goals. I told them that if they could write them down if it was something they wanted to achieve in the future, the brain stimulates you into action.

In the UK, if we're stagnating in our jobs, we often motivate ourselves by writing down our goals – so I encouraged the children to write theirs down too. Silly me, I asked the 25 children to write down three goals each, and 30 minutes later they hadn't finished, then I realised that they only had one pencil between them and that they were waiting patiently in turn. That made me bring pens and paper to my future visits. I told them that if they wrote their goals down and turned up the next evening, then I would have been to Mombasa to buy three footballs. They loved to play football on the beach, but their ball was a bundle of rags tied up with coconut string.

The next night I arrived with the footballs, and, silly me, the tide was in. The boys lived on the other side of the bay, it was going dark, I was just about to leave when I thought I saw a head bobbing up and down in the sea – I looked again, and sure enough, it was a head, then I spotted another and another! My heart froze, the boys were swimming in the rough waves across the bay to get their footballs. My heart was pounding, with the waves and the current, I was worried sick. But sure enough, every one of them came safely out of the sea. They were shouting 'Papa John, Papa John,' and I hugged them all. They could have gone missing, been sucked under by the currents, and that would have been it, that was the cruelty of life! I started to wonder if something had happened to Grasshopper, that little boy who ran into school at the age of seven. We looked and looked but again didn't find Grasshopper.

The third year, we were praying that Grasshopper would have returned, but still no Grasshopper. "Sorry, Papa John," the villagers said, "No Grasshopper, we cannot find him." We couldn't look, we had other responsibilities, viable water wells needed to be found, so the ladies didn't have to walk further and further out of the village. The rainy season was in, more and more children needed educating. Our days were busy and enjoyable, but still, we missed Grasshopper.

The fourth year we returned with more funding for the villagers, and I remember the beautiful businesspeople, and people of Liverpool donated money. We bought them rice and food, we fed two thousand of them – they were so happy to see the rice we nearly got crushed when they rushed forward to get it, they were so excited. The villagers were grateful and happy, but no Grasshopper!

Two mornings before we were ready to leave for Manchester, I was walking along the beach as I had all those many years ago. It was 6 am, and I was taking time out when suddenly, I heard a voice screaming out, "Papa John, Papa John," and I looked along the beach, and I could see a figure shouting and waving, and suddenly, there he was – Grasshopper! Instead of me running away as I did many years ago, I ran to meet him, and we hugged each other tightly. I was so relieved, I looked at him, and in a way, I felt like an angry father confronting his daughter when she sneaks in at 4 am after a night out.

"Where have you been then? I've been worried sick; you should have let me know." I looked at him, and realised he was now age 18, a grown man; he was different, tall and muscular.

He said, "Papa John sit down, I tell you a story."

I laughed, every time I came here, I ended up sitting on the same rocks telling a story – but now it was Grasshoppers turn!

As I sat listening to his story, about what he had been doing over the last four years, I realised that we don't have time to reinvent the wheel, why go through life making the same mistakes, the same bad decisions.

The top gurus in life say – 'Listen to the experts.'

They have already made mistakes, but they found success methods. That's why most people should have their own mentors, people with experience in life and business. You can learn from anybody; they don't have to be a university professor or an expert, or top leader. You can learn from the young, the poor, the underprivileged; your mind is open to anything, and the story Grasshopper told me I assure you, it changed my life, and it made me re-evaluate everything. I learned more from this young man, whom I had known since he was seven than I'd learnt from many books I had read, and many experts that had given me advice. I was stunned, shocked, delighted and amazed!

This is what he told me, "Papa John, I got to think about the story about the acres of diamonds and the old man who left his family; but you said the acres of diamonds were already under his feet, not only diamonds, you said I needed to find my diamonds, my music inside, the things that I'm good at doing and the skills that God blessed me with to have a happy life. So, Papa John, I started to think, what is Grasshoppers main strength, what is his one skill he has, and Grasshopper realised Papa John that I'm not good at many things, so I searched and thought until I realised what I was my number one skill."

You see, all of us go through life with this skill, knowledge and ability and they say that most people never take the time or make an effort to find out what they are really good at doing, Grasshopper did. I've said before that we all have this incredible music inside us, but around 85% of the population will go to their grave with the music still inside, never having taken the time to make the most of the skills that they had been born with.

I said, "Grasshopper, tell me, pray tell me, what is your acres of diamonds?"

"Papa John," he said, "my music inside is..."

I waited, expectantly.

"Somersaulting, Grasshopper is good at somersaulting. I'm very happy somersaulting, and I wake up happy every morning!"

I was stunned! I expected something else, something more. "So, Grasshopper, what did you do with this skill?"

If you find something you love, that's a hobby sometimes you have to find a way to turn that hobby into a way of making money. He'd only wanted to pay for his education and keep a roof over his family's head.

He replied, "Papa John, I looked for other boys in the village and told them about the music and acres of diamonds, and I found five more boys whose skill was also somersaulting, we all love somersaulting."

"So," he said, making me smile, "We decide to form a team called the Grasshopper Somersault Team, and we started to practice every day to be very good."

It is said that if you find something you are good at, you need to develop it and develop muscle memory, you have to learn about it. To be excellent in your business and your career, you need to find the skills.

Let's use sales as an example, give yourself an honest score from 1-10, one being bad, five being average, ten being excellent. Take time to evaluate and reflect on your answer.

Even if you score six, you need to go away and practice your sales skills! Prospecting, identifying the need, presentation, closing the sale, overcoming objections, asking for referrals. The top salespeople around the world that earn millions every year have done so by practising their skills daily – and that's what Grasshopper did!

"Papa John," he said, "You say that everyone likes the nice things in life, but no one wants to pay the price, so we pay the price and practice seven days a week."

"Seven days a week," I gasped. "Good on you, Grasshopper, what time of day?"

"As soon as the sun rises, we start practising our somersaulting, until the sun sets, and then we rest. We love it, Papa John, we have been doing it for years, we are very good."

He blew me away with his next comments. "Papa John, we know we are very good, but we wanted to earn money for our families and education."

It transpired that they realised that no one in the village had the money to pay to watch them somersault, so they left, they had heard that many miles away in the big tourist hotels in Kenya that they could be paid to entertain tourists from all over the world. Now I realised why he had been gone so long.

"How did you get there?" I asked.

"Papa John, we walked the Coast Road."

My mind suddenly realised, most people who lose their jobs and can't support their families, instead of asking, where is there a location, where is a city where I can find work, or they might appreciate my skills and knowledge? They do nothing. Sometimes you have to get out of your comfort zone and move, to support your family, and this is exactly what Grasshopper was doing. He had to leave behind the people that he grew up with for one reason – to earn money for his family.

'Papa John, we slept under the stars and caught fish to eat, we were very tired, and after six months, Papa John, we were very excited to reach the big hotels. We tried the first hotel, but the guards wouldn't let us in. We felt rejected, but we stayed for many days asking for the manager each time.'

They had overcome the rejection and persevered. But they kept believing and had confident expectations that the manager would come out eventually. Everything happens for a reason, and the manager (after hearing about them for six weeks), had come out to tell them to go home.

"We are the famous Grasshopper Somersault Team," they said, "Can we come into your hotel to show you and your guests our somersaults." It was a presentation they had rehearsed for months!

"No." The manager had replied, "You can stay outside the hotel and do your somersaulting there - goodbye."

They had realised then that it was an opportunity to show off their skills. So, they waited until the tourists had come out. In short, they did their own market research.

Every time you have a new product, or invention, you need to find out before you put too much investment into it; will people pay for it? Do they want it? Where will you sell your product? So, they watched the comings and goings of the tourists and figured out that they were coming out after breakfast and lunch, to sit on the beach, and for an evening stroll.

"So, Papa John, we started somersaulting three times a day outside the hotel, the tourists, liked and clapped us, so I quickly got a coconut shell and put it there for tourists to put money in, and they liked us, they kept coming to see us! They put money in, and soon the hotel manager came out and invited us into the hotel to be their evening cabaret act."

"What did you do with the money Grasshopper?" I asked him.

"We saved, we hid it under a rock, we saved."

So, unlike most of us, money burns a hole in our pocket, Grasshopper, and his team, had saved. It violates Parkinson's Law, which suggests that we spend to meet our income!

"Anyway, Papa John, we got good money, and another hotel, invited us to somersault outside, and suddenly, Papa John, we were very busy working early morning until late at night."

"When we found we had enough money, we started the long journey home."

"So, hold on Grasshopper, what you're telling me is that you found your music inside, found your acres of diamonds, practised and practised until you were excellent, then you walked hundreds of miles to find paid work, to find people who loved what you do, you did your market research and did your somersaults! And all the time you ran mean and lean, you didn't spend unnecessarily, you saved every penny. Grasshopper." I exclaimed, "That's leadership."

That was entrepreneurialism at the highest level. I was in awe!! These young boys had given me a lesson in business; I need to improve myself, get out of my comfort zone in unconscious incompetence, go back to my Academy and learn more skills and earn more money.

"And yesterday, Papa John, we came back to the village."

"Grasshopper, I'm in awe! What are you going to do now?"

"Grasshopper now has enough money, to get the roof fixed for my family so that they can sleep comfortably at night."

"What else will you do with the money?"

"I go to Mombasa tomorrow; Grasshopper has saved enough money for two years of college."

I nearly fell off my rock. I couldn't believe it, not only had he found his acres of diamonds, he worked on his skills, he had a goal, he had a target – and he achieved it! It was quite remarkable, where most people fail at doing anything like that as they have no self-discipline, I was in awe!!

"Grasshopper, that's marvellous."

My heart was pounding as I'd learnt new knowledge off Grasshopper.

"What else is happening, Grasshopper?"

Suddenly he blushed!

"Papa John, I said I wanted to build the straw roof, I wanted to go to college in Mombasa and, Papa John, I didn't have to come to Liverpool to meet a lovely girl and fall in love. Grasshopper has fallen in love with a beautiful Kenyan girl," he said blushing.

"Well done, Grasshopper."

I was in awe because he had more self-discipline than me! More courage, more vision, he wasn't going to give up. They say most people who have big goals, big dreams, when it gets difficult, just give up. Grasshopper had proven to me that he had tremendous willpower and self-discipline.

I read years later; it was Elbert Hubbard, a twentieth-century writer, who wrote 'Self-discipline is the ability to make yourself do what you should do when you should do it, whether you feel like it or not.' I'd grown from then, and Grasshopper proved that to me, you see, self-discipline is the iron quality of character, it is the foundation of integrity and courage, your level of self-discipline has a major impact on what you accomplish in every area of your life and endeavours. I've just realised over the years that other definitions of self-discipline are self-mastery and self-control, and control is a critical element of happiness. Grasshopper was so happy; you see you feel good about yourself when you feel that you are in control of your own life. He was in control of his life.

When you make a decision to do, or to refrain from doing, something and you discipline yourself to stick to your resolution, even when you don't feel like it, you feel much better about yourself, you feel in control. I just realised now, that there's a correlation between self-discipline and self-esteem, the more you discipline yourself to do the things that you have resolved to do the more you like and respect yourself. The more you respect yourself, the more capable you become of disciplining yourself to do the things that you know that you should do. Each quality reinforces the others, as Grasshopper and his somersault team had demonstrated to me. No, he hadn't been to university or college yet, and he came from a humble background, but these were his own core values, and I sat open-mouthed realising that I'd just had one of the best education sessions of my life.

He said, "Papa John, before you and Mama Linda go back on the big white plane to Liverpool, can Grasshopper and his team give you a demonstration?"

"Yes Grasshopper, I want to see you perform, with your music inside and your acres of diamonds!"

"Papa John, can you bring Mama Linda at 5 pm to the beach tonight?"

I went back to the hotel to tell Linda that I had found Grasshopper.

"He's alive, he's well, he had a fantastic story to tell, and he wants to meet us on the beach at 5 pm, to show us his acres of diamonds, and his music inside." I told her.

We couldn't get there fast enough; we were there by 5 pm with a big camcorder to record every second of it, I felt like Spielberg directing them to where I could film without the sun in my eyes.

I can say, I've never seen anything like what they did, they weren't just a somersault team, they were like birds flying through the air, it was amazing. Talk about the X-factor; they were tremendous, their acrobatics were unbelievable. I was shaking so much I had to ask Linda to take the camera!

I was still in awe, and as we were watching passing jeeps stopped, full of tourist who wanted to watch, the tourists ran across the beach clapping and whooping because it was breathtaking! It was almost impossible to achieve. I've never seen anything like it since. Grasshopper, being the perfect entrepreneur, put his coconut shell out for the tourists to contribute! French, German, British tourists, all clapped, blown away by this amazing entertainment.

Grasshopper asked us at the end "Papa John, Mama Linda, did you like it?"

Tears came to my eyes; this was the young man who dodged Joseph, the headmaster, to get into class, he wouldn't give up; he believed in education. And this was the young man who went through school and was at the age of 14 was looking after his family and took full responsibility. He had a goal and a vision to give his family a better life, a better straw roof, he wanted to educate himself, and he walked hundreds of miles to earn enough money for his own education. This young man had found his music inside; I gave him the biggest hug ever.

Even now, when we go back to this beautiful village, we see Grasshopper now, and I'm delighted to say that he's one of the village elders. Everybody respects Grasshopper, he's now a role model, and tells all the stories I told him. I can say, he's got a bit beyond himself. I tell this story when I'm in Mombasa to all the local officials and the Lord Mayor, and around Kenya where I go to give my talks, and they are all in awe of Grasshopper, they visit the village just to see Grasshopper and his somersault team. The reason I say that he's got beyond himself is that the last time I visited, I was walking along the beach early in the morning and Grasshopper was walking towards me, he'd been to Mombasa the day before to have a t-shirt made, and on the t-shirt it said 'I am the famous Grasshopper.'

I said, "You cheeky little thing." And hugged him.

That experience changed my values, changed my life; it was synchronicity. I was glad; I was so glad I made the mistake of booking the wrong holiday. I can look back on my life and say that if I hadn't have done this, made my mistake; I wouldn't be where I am today. So, Grasshopper, God bless you.

10. FLY WITH THE EAGLES

As I said at the beginning of my Kenyan story, there I was in the middle of Mombasa, in a warring country. Kenya had erupted in political warfare, with tribes warring with other tribes. My villagers had asked me to go with them to help bring peace to their beloved country. At least my villagers were not at war with each other. There were different religions, different sectors; but there I was sitting there – one of the few white men around, and they noticed me there; someone tapped me on the shoulder and asked, "Are you Papa John from England?"

"Yes," I replied.

"Would you give a speech about your thoughts on Kenya, Papa John?"

Wow, I was supposed to be keeping a low profile, the British Government had said Kenya was a no-go zone.

'Yes,' I replied, thinking I would have some time to prepare a speech.

Suddenly, the speakers boomed out, "Our next speaker is Papa John, from England."

People looked around in amazement, Grasshopper and the villagers were jumping up and down with excitement. Warily, with my heart pounding, walked onto the stage. There must have been about 5000 people there all just staring at me; they had wired speakers throughout Mombasa so that the people who couldn't get close to the stadium could still hear. Suddenly, the American TV reporters, the BBC, all come alive – there was a white man walking out to speak. The cameras were focussed on me, my heart was pounding, and I wondered what I would say.

When you get taught in public speaking, you learn that if you start to get nervous or panic the right-brain switches off, that's why people become blubbering wrecks. I knew that I needed to stay positive as I walked onto the stage. Using the affirmations that I was taught years ago, 'I can do it, I can do it, I am the best, I am the best,' helped me keep my right-brain from switching off. I got to the floor mikes; I could even see the representatives from the United Nations looking on in amazement, that I was even in Mombasa, or had even come to the stadium, where the tribes were hating each other.

"Papa John," I was asked, "What do you really feel about Kenya? Apparently, you have been coming here for 15 years, what are your thoughts?"

Suddenly, the cameras and the microphones homed in on me. Sometimes in life, you just have to let your inner voice out and talk. Nothing was prepared, but I looked at them all and knew I had to use my public speaking skills, making eye contact, making your voice loud and clear with the right body language. My talk only lasted a few minutes, but it went down so well that they played it on the news, on Kenyan television for the next seven days. The words that came out of my mouth I couldn't believe until I watched it back later.

I said, "I am from Liverpool, and I have been coming to Kenya for 15 years, and I love this country, you have values, you have heart, you have discipline, and you are the nicest people I have ever met in my life." I continued "How dare you let me down, all this fighting and killing has got to stop. You are my role models, and I can't believe what you are doing to each other. Please, the world is watching you right now, you don't want this as your legacy for your grandchildren to learn about, about how you killed and maimed each other. Please, come back and show the world that you are a family, have forgiveness in your heart, all of us have got to go forward. We Brits admire you Kenyans, you were once a part of our colony, and we don't want you to fight anymore, so come on! I love the village I go to, and I'll always come back, and I'll always respect you, so listen, from the bottom of my heart I want you to forgive each other." I finished off by saying, "All of us have got to believe in a great future, we've got to be happy, and I want you all right now to make a pledge to me and all of my villagers that from now, you are going to put your weapons down and you're going to fly with the eagles, and no more scratching like nasty turkeys. Will you make a pledge? Will you say for me right now, everybody – fly with the eagles."

To my amazement a roar went up, "FLY WITH THE EAGLES NO SCRATCHING WITH THE TURKEYS!" and they were all laughing!

"Once more!" I said. I got them to repeat it four more times, along with "We are Kenyans, we are brothers, we are flying with the eagles," followed by a tremendous roar, even outside the stadium.

I said, "I love you all, and God bless you, you are my special eagles."

The stadium erupted, I was shaking, I didn't know how to leave the stage, and everyone was hugging, and one of the United Nations representatives came over to congratulate me saying; "Mr Haynes, that was one of the most amazing speeches I have heard."

My speech was televised all around Kenya!

It was nothing to do with me, but I know that a peaceful resolution was found two days later, and I hoped I'd helped a tiny bit. But those Kenyans came together, and it's been good ever since. That, possibly, has been one of the highlights of my life.

Anyway, we went back to the village with Grasshopper and the village elders, we had a party, and we celebrated. It was quite funny; they invited me, and as we were all sitting around, one of the villagers asked, "Papa John, would you like a strong drink?"

So, he climbed up a coconut tree, chops off a coconut and brought it down, opens it up, and offered it to me, I got very drunk! The alcohol content was very high, so high I was singing.

The following day I was leaving. Once again, it was a sad situation, people talking about my speech, people were excited, and I felt that I'd done something right in my life for once. Not only had I helped establish water wells, and found Grasshopper,

I'd also tried to unite a country. But I was so sad to leave; with the average age of death being between 40-50, that next year when I came back, some of my closest friends, my dear loved ones, will have died.

Every time we leave, all the villagers come to see us off, sometimes as many as two thousand, and every time I stand up in the jeep and ask them three questions. I shout out, "I loved it, I'll be back next year, I won't let you down, and here are my three questions."

"What are you?" I shout.

They shout back "Unstoppable!"

These are villagers have very little food, shelter, water, schooling, but they always answer "Unstoppable!"

"How do you feel?" I ask, always with a lump in my throat; how do you feel?

They are starving they have very little, but they all shout back, "Fantastic!"

They mean it, they jump up and down, they really mean it. "Fantastic!"

The last question is this, "And what are you doing?"

They all put their hands in the air and shout happily, "Flying with the Eagles!"

I wave and blow kisses as my jeep takes off down the dirt track, I have tears in my eyes. These are my true brothers and sisters, everyone waves, and the kids run after the jeep until we disappear into the distance. Once again synchronicity and serendipity; it happened for a reason. Even now I send money and get back as often as I can. It's changed my life, and made me the person that I am today, so all of you right now, I'll ask you these three questions, stand up now, and I'll say to you:

"What are you?"

Now shout back, from the bottom of your heart, for your family, "I'm Unstoppable!"

Now I'm going to ask, "How do you feel?" and here you are going to scream out, for your life, for your family, "I feel Fantastic!"

And then my last question to you all is, "And what are you doing?"

Don't forget that eagles are people like you, they love their families, and have confident expectations; so, you'll shout back to me "Flying with the Eagles!"

So that's my Kenyan story, learn from it, grow from it, always give to other people and please, please, please; fly with the fantastic eagles!

IN REFLECTION

I t is said that your outer world reflects your inner world. My inner world was one of low self-esteem, low self-worth, and low self-confidence. I felt like a laughing-stock, and this reflected in my outer world in the form of self-pity, anger, blame, learned helplessness and frequent tears of desperation. Mental fitness is in a way the same thing as physical fitness. Both forms require regular training. Just as you undertake regular physical activity to keep your body strong and healthy, mental fitness is brought about by exercising the mind. Years later, I was introduced to the activities required to enjoy mental fitness.

- You must first take full responsibility for your own situation. The current state of your life, your career and your family is down to you. Get out of the Valley of Blame and remember the saying - *If it is to be, it is up to me!*
- Be the master of change and not the victim of change. If you are unhappy with some aspect of your life or indeed your entire life, you must do something about it. Rest assured that no-one else will.
- Keep a list of written goals and clear accompanying plans as to how you will achieve them.
- Recognised that increased skills and knowledge is the key to get you out of debt and give you a good standard of living. Identify what skills and knowledge you need and get out there and learn.
- Commit yourself to personal mastery in your career. It is not enough to be mediocre. You must be excellent at what you do. Excellence will open doors

for you.

- Use positive self-talk and affirmations to keep you feeling mindful and make your immune system a force to be reckoned with.
- Visualise the things you wish to have or do in your life. Do this daily. Avoid thinking about or visualising the things you don't want in your life.

These activities will help you to achieve mental fitness. If only I had known back then what I am so blessed to know now.

MY MEMORIES

Training and motivating the children in Kenya.

Can you spot Grasshopper?

The famous Hygena Team presented me with this after winning so many cups - even in those days I looked old!

A picture of the water well provided to help the people of Kenya.

In Mombasa, before my big speech. Liverpool Football Club are known everywhere!

Giving sweets to the starving kids in Kenya.

Kenyan Villagers show their appreciation for the water well.

My Dad - who would always share his WW2 stories with me.